Sir Robert Seppings
of Fakenham

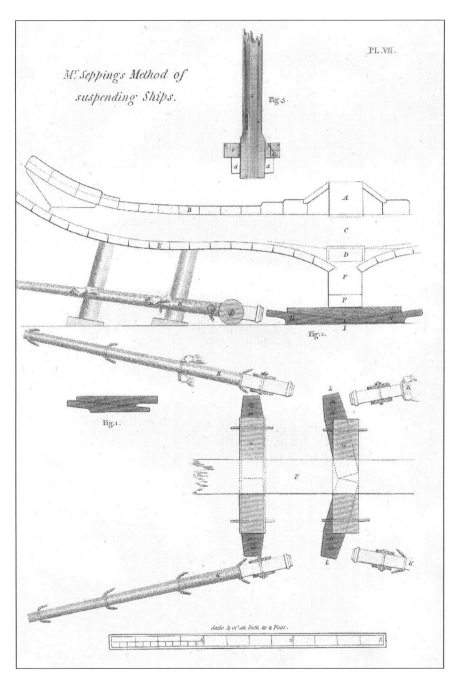

Mr. Sepping's Method of suspending Ships.

Seppings' Blocks.

Sir Robert Seppings of Fakenham

From Rural Messenger Boy to Surveyor of the King's Navy

Peter Elphick

POPPYLAND
PUBLISHING

Published by Poppyland Publishing, Lowestoft, NR32 3BB, 2022.
ISBN 978-1-909796-93-5
Design and production by Guy Myles Warren.

Contents

Author's Acknowledgements		*vii*
List of Illustrations		*ix*
Foreword		1
1	From Childhood to Dockyard Shipwright	3
2	At Plymouth Dockyard: The Beginnings of Invention and of Controversy	14
3	Master Shipwright, Chatham Dockyard	25
4	Surveyor of the King's Navy	35
5	Some Protégés and Followers: His Relationship with the School of Naval Architecture	48
6	Sir Robert and the Timber Problem	58
7	Steam ships and Experimental Squadrons	73
8	The Last Years in Office	91
9	Unquiet Retirement: the Acrimonious Correspondence with Captain Frederick Marryat	97
10	The Final Years	105
11	In Memoriam	110
	Appendix I	114
	Appendix II	120
	Bibliography	126
	Index	131

For Eunice, who made everything happen.

Author's Acknowledgements

Sincere thanks are due to the following persons and organisations for their generous and friendly help during the research for this book.

Dr. Alan Lemmers for permission to use substantial quotes from one of his learned works, and for supplying copies of two pictures and their captions.

Members of the staff of the Caird Library, National Maritime Museum, Greenwich, for permission to use information contained in the papers of Brigadier J.J. Packard in MSS/76/016. Use has also been made of Mrs. Faith Packard's book entitled *Our Family History*. In both of these cases every effort has been made to trace direct descendants of Brigadier and Mrs. Packard in order to request permissions, but none have yet been traced.

The staff of the Norfolk Library & Information Services and particularly the ladies of the Fakenham branch, for their unfailing kindness and patience.

Ann Bligh; the Rev. Rod Cork, Vicar of St. Mary Magdalene Church, Taunton for pictures of the Seppings' memorial items in the church, and for permission to use them; Louise Harrison, London Metropolitan Archives; Lt. Colonel R.C. Cole Mackintosh, Clerk to the Worshipful Company of Shipwrights; Mrs. Felicity Randall; Sue Webber, Collections Officer, Elmsbridge Museum, Surrey; Vikki Mulford, Digital Engagement Officer of the Chatham Historic Dockyard Trust.

Excerpts from *Mr. Robert Seppings (1805) XXXVI, Method of obviating the necessity of lifting ships*, Philosophical Magazine Series 1, 22:87, 242-247, together with the associated diagram, appear by permission of Taylor & Francis Ltd.

Excerpts from the Lord Liverpool Papers Ms. 38.368 appear by permission of the British Library.

Quotations from Admiralty documents in the National Archives under Crown copyright appear by permission of HMSO.

Three internet sources have proved valuable in the search for Seppings' family details: the Turnbull Clan Genealogy Collection, the HathiTrust Digital Library administered by the Indiana University and the University of Michigan; and the Seppings Family History website.

Special mention is due to Mrs. Christine Colthurst for permission to use quotations and pictures from the Seppings' material collected by her late husband Christopher, a direct descendant of Lt. John Milligen Seppings R.N.; and to her daughter Dr. Sarah Patel, and granddaughter Ella who helped in accessing the material from storage.

Special mention must also be made to my friend Guy Warren, who set up and designed this book for publication.

List of Illustrations

Cover: Portrait of Sir Robert Seppings, Surveyor of the Royal Navy. Oil painting by John Prescott Knight. (*Courtesy of Mrs. Christine Colthurst.*)

Frontispiece: Stepping's Blocks (*Philosophic Magazine.*)

1 Robert Seppings as a young boy. (*Seppings' family image.*)
2 Mrs. Lydia Seppings, Sir Robert's mother. Pencil sketch by a shipwright at Chatham, circa 1810 (*Seppings' family image.*)
3 Robert Seppings' birthplace in Holt Road, Fakenham. Now called Anchor House it has been extensively altered over the years. (*Author's image.*)
4 Memorial 'bride and groom' chairs dedicated to Sir Robert and Lady Seppings in St. Mary Magdalene Church, Taunton. (*Courtesy of Rev. Rod Cork, Vicar of that Church.*)
5 Some of the gifts presented to Sir Robert Seppings by Foreign Heads of State.
6 Coat of Arms of Sir Robert Seppings.
7 Embroidered depiction of Vivary, Sir Robert's home in Taunton.
8 Diagram showing the main differences between the Seppings and Snodgrass methods of strengthening ship structures.
9 The 'Swan-Necked' Miss Louisa Seppings.
10 Portrait of Gabriel Snodgrass, Surveyor to the East India Company. (*European Magazine.*)
11 Portrait of F.C. Hohlenberg, Danish Naval Architect (1765-1804) (*Private collection.*)
12 Portrait of Captain William May, Dockyard Superintendent of the Amsterdam Admiralty (1725-1807) (*Private collection.*)
13 Portrait of John Milligen Seppings, Shipbuilder and Inspector of Shipping, East India Company at Calcutta. Son of Sir Robert Seppings. (*Courtesy of Mrs. Christine Colthurst.*)
14 Portrait of Marianne Seppings nee Matthews, m. John Milligen Seppings at Calcutta, 1823. (*Courtesy of Mrs. Christine Colthurst.*)
15 The framing of Seppings' Circular Stern, compared with the conventional Transom Stern.
16 Portrait of Captain Edward James Seppings, H.E.I.C. Army, son of John Milligen and Marianne Seppings. Killed at the Massacre at Cawnpore. Grandson of Sir Robert Seppings. (*Courtesy of Mrs. Christine Colthurst.*)
17 Portrait of Lt. John Milligen Seppings R.N., Controller of Revenue Cutters. Sir Robert Seppings brother. (*Courtesy of Mrs, Christine Colthurst.*)

18 Engraving of the Danish-built ship Christian VII, showing the
    May-Hohlenberg pinched-in stern. After this ship was captured by the
    Royal Navy, British shipwrights found this style of stern both 'curious
    and interesting'. (*Naval Chronicle.*)
19 HMS Victory. (*From an old photograph, private collection.*)
20 HMS Victory under Jury Rig entering Gibraltar Bay after the Battle
    of Trafalgar. (*Private collection.*)
21 HMS Unicorn preserved at Dundee. (*Author's collection.*)
22 Seppings' Iron Knees in HMS Unicorn. (*Private collection.*)
23 Exterior Chatham No.3 Slipway, Seppings' Shed. (*Courtesy, Chatham
    Historic Dockyard Trust.*)
24 Interior Chatham No.3 Slipway, Seppings' Shed. (*Courtesy, Chatham
    Historic Dockyard Trust.*)
25 Drawings of Seppings' Blocks. (*Philosophic Magazine.*)
26 The Fakenham Town sign. The depicted ship, is in honour of Sir Robert
    Seppings. (*Author's collection.*)
27 One of the facsimile printer's blocks in Fakenham Market Place,
    honouring Sir Robert Seppings. (*Author's collection.*)

Foreword

The inventions and improvements in shipbuilding techniques and dockyard operations introduced in Britain in the early 19th century by Sir Robert Seppings, can be said to have provided the final major evolutionary changes in the era of timber-built sailing warships. During his time in the post of Surveyor of the Navy, Seppings also played a significant role in the substitution of iron for wood in some ship structures, and was responsible for designing the Royal Navy's very first but largely forgotten steam-driven vessel, the *Congo*, forgotten because it was never commissioned as such into the navy. (Later, the navy's first *commissioned* steamship, HMS *Comet*, was also designed by him.) Thirteen years before his elevation to the post of Surveyor, Seppings made his name by inventing a method that considerably eased the problem of gaining access for repair purposes to the bottom parts of ships in dry-dock, a method that did away with the previous need to use hundreds of men manning back-breaking lifting devices. We shall see that some of his improvements, the strengthening of ships' bows for example, must have saved many seamens' lives. His innovations were not however confined to shipbuilding and ship repairing par se, for some dealt with ancillary naval matters concerning, for instance, the safe mooring of laid-up ships (in naval parlance those ships lying in Ordinary) and their expeditious unmooring when they were required again.

Seppings once wrote, "It is the fate of the most important and beneficial improvements, on their first introduction, to meet with opposition from some quarter or other; and more especially if they should happen to differ from long established usage". However, we shall see that it was not only that which caused his professional life to be filled with controversy, a situation that was to some degree illustrated by a paragraph written in 1828 by Sir John Barrow, the Second Secretary of the Admiralty, describing his own official visit to the Dutch Naval Dockyard in Rotterdam. '*Under a second roof was a fifty-gun frigate building, and under a third, one of the same class repairing. The new frigate had a round stern, similar to which Sir Robert Seppings was accused of having pilfered from the Dutch...*' (Barrow went on to absolve his friend Seppings of that particular charge by listing a number of differences between the two types of stern.)

Most of Seppings' inventions and innovations began as experiments and were improved as time went on. The introduction of his diagonal framing system was, in his own words, "the cause of a total change in our national bulwark", and he was not exaggerating. He possessed the force of personality necessary to get permission from a usually hide-bound Admiralty to conduct what he called 'severe trials' for some of his inventions to a much greater extent than had any of his predecessors, and he followed them through with personal observation. In some instances, that process took a number of years. In consequence it has not been possible to write this work in a strictly chronological way; often it has been necessary to skip forward and then back again to give a coherent picture. It is hoped that the injection, where appropriate, of events in Seppings' family history has helped in this process.

Despite his tendency towards controversy, he was arguably the ablest of all the men who down the years held the post of Surveyor of the Navy and was amongst the greatest builders ever to construct wooden ships. Another important fact is that, at a time when Britain was being threatened by French invasion forces poised on the other side of the Channel, his early work on improving dry docking operations resulted in much faster turn-round times for ships in port undergoing repair and maintenance. During this period the navy was always short of ships, so the reductions in the times they spent in port, estimated by contemporaries as being up to fifty per cent in many cases, contributed significantly to the fact that the Royal Navy managed not only to forestall Bonaparte's invasion plans, but also to wreck most of his other maritime ventures.

1
The Beginnings: From Childhood to Dockyard Shipwright

On the face of it, a boy born in 1767 in the small market town of Fakenham in rural Norfolk, was an unlikely candidate to later hold the most important shipbuilding post in the Royal Navy and one day to be knighted for his services. That might be considered even more unlikely when one learns that the lad concerned stemmed from a long-established line of yeoman farmers, no recorded direct member of which had previously had anything at all to do with the sea or ships apart from an obscure lieutenant (who like our hero was called Robert Seppings) who passed the examination for that naval rank in 1704 before completely disappearing from the records.[1]

Our Robert Seppings was born in a house, now called Anchor House (and which has been altered somewhat), in Holt Road, Fakenham on 11 December 1767. Baptised in the Parish Church of St. Peter and St. Paul on 24 January following, he was the fifth of seven children of Robert Seppings senior and his wife Lydia, daughter of a linen-draper called John Milligen from over the county line in Harleston, Suffolk. The couple were married in the Fakenham church on 29 January 1760. Their first child called John was born in December of that year but survived for only a few weeks. The others were Lydia born in 1762, Mary in 1763, Helen in 1765, then our Robert, followed by John Milligen in 1770, and the youngest called Elizabeth in 1774.

Robert Seppings senior seems to have been a rather feckless individual for, as the eldest of four siblings, one supposes he should one day have taken over his father's farm, but instead he became a cattle salesman and not a very successful one at that. It could be said that Lydia had married somewhat beneath her social status as her father had made such a success of his business that, 'he was able to retire and set himself up as a landed gentleman in Shouldham', a village in Norfolk south of King's Lynn.[2] One of Lydia's brothers called John after their father, had joined the Navy in about 1739 and had risen to the rank of captain, a connection that later came to define young Robert's life.

---

[1] Syrett, *Commissioned Sea Officers of the Royal Navy.*
[2] See papers of J.J. Packard in MSS/76/016, National Maritime Museum. Brigadier Packard's wife Faith, was a direct Seppings descendant through a female line.

The surname Seppings is unusual. One authority states that it derived from 'seven-pence' or 'sevenpenny', and may first have been the nickname given to a pedlar who repeatedly shouted out the price of his wares. Another authority says it stemmed from a description of someone not very tall. The Sepens and Sepings variants of the name have been found in documents dating from 1524 and 1674. Although the name was never confined to Norfolk, by the middle of the 18th century there were Seppings families all over that county with a seemingly large concentration around the Hundreds of Gallow and North Greenhoe at such places as Hempton, Fulmodeston, West Rainham, Syderstone, South Creake, Barney and Wells-next-the-Sea as well as at Fakenham. It was sometimes used as a first Christian name, for according to Pigot's Directory, in the 1830s a man called Seppings Hook, ran a school at the Buttlands in Wells. (We shall see that Seppings, and the surname Milligen – in the case of the latter beginning with Robert's brother John Milligen – became favoured second Christian names for many members of the family.) Whites Directory of 1841 recorded a Thomas Seppings farming at Whitehall, near Syderstone. Further afield, a certain William Seppings was Mayor of King's Lynn in 1848 and again in 1855: in 1844 he was a member of the Committee behind the Prospectus for the Lynn and Dereham Railway Company. (See *Railway Chronicle* for that year.) One of his sons, Thomas Johnson Seppings, also became Mayor of that town in 1878, and another son, William Seppings who died in 1895 aged 54, was a noted solicitor of that place.

It is not known how young Robert gained his early education, but one of some sort he did get in an age when formal education was far from universal. (One can venture a guess that he might have been taught by his mother who had probably received a good education paid for by her father.) Anyway, however it was obtained, later evidence suggests that it was considerably more than just adequate. A descendant once wrote that Robert never knew much about, nor indeed cared much for, any branch of mathematics apart from arithmetic.[3] We shall see as we describe some of his achievements, that that was unlikely to have been the case. Whatever early education he received,

---

[3] Edward Milligen Beloe, in the Seppings' entry in the first edition of the *Dictionary of National Biography* (DNB) 1885-1900. He was a Seppings' descendant through a female line.

it would have been curtailed when he was twelve for in 1780 his father fell upon hard times and that resulted in some radical changes in the family. Young Robert had to find a way to supplement the family's income, and with the first recorded sign of the energy and resourcefulness he was to exhibit throughout his later professional life, he began a mail service from Fakenham to Wells-next-the-Sea transporting letters by mule possibly along the route between the two towns now known as the 'Dry Road', then a mere track. In his multi-volume *History of Norfolk*, Francis Blomefield wrote that, 'The merchants of the sea port of Wells, constantly attended [Fakenham corn sales] to buy corn of the farmers for exportation'. Perhaps young Robert carried mail pertaining to such purchases – contracts, cargo manifests, bills of lading etc., and, as many Wells' merchants and shipowners had premises on the quayside, maybe that was how he gained an initial interest in ships. At Wells there were also a number of small but busy shipyards that he might have found of interest.

Despite young Robert's efforts to help out, so precarious had the family's finances become by October 1780, that Mrs. Seppings persuaded her brother, the childless Captain John Milligen R.N. and his wife Martha (who was living in Plymouth), who had already adopted the two orphaned daughters called Martha (born 1766) and Charlotte (born 1774) of a brother called Thomas Milligen (who had died at Shouldham a few years earlier), to adopt two of her children, Lydia aged 17, and John Milligen aged 10.[4]

Robert Seppings senior died in the late summer of 1781. Aged only forty-eight, he was buried in Fakenham churchyard on 10 September of that year. That event led to the end of young Robert's mail by mule efforts and to a further breaking up of the family home when the now Widow Seppings asked Captain Milligen also to adopt 15-year old Robert, a move that took place in 1782.

Captain John Milligen (c1728-1788) was not one of those great British naval commanders who illuminated the 18th century naval scene, men whose names like those of Nelson, Rodney, Hood, Berry, Jervis, Collingwood, Fremantle, Foley and Hardy, have resounded down the years. Rather, he

---

[4] See Packard papers: letter from S. Person of London, who was Captain Milligen's London agent, to Robert Seppings senior dated 11 October 1780.

was amongst those who formed the great majority of sea commanders, men who were honourable and capable but not brilliant, and who perhaps had not managed to find a patron to dispense what was then called 'interest' on their behalf, something that was very important for career advancement in the navy of those days. Milligen had passed his lieutenant's examination on 24 June 1746 and is known to have served in that rank in HMS *Eagle* in 1755-1756. He was promoted commander in 1761 and then to post-captain in 1768, and commanded a 32-gun frigate in 1776/1777 in American waters during the War of Independence. That was a steady but by no means outstanding rate of progress through the commissioned ranks. His last command, which began in July 1778, was of the old 60-gun two-decker HMS *Dunkirk* built at Woolwich twenty-three years earlier. Unfit for further sea service the ship was stationed in The Downs off Deal and used in what was called 'Harbour Service' which included acting as a floating gun battery to protect that important anchorage, and as a Receiving Ship for holding victims of the Press Gang before they were allocated to sea-going vessels. Milligen remained in command of *Dunkirk* until 1782, when he retired to live with his wife and adopted family at Plymouth.

In 1780 Captain Milligen dispensed some of his own stock of 'interest' on his nephew, the adopted 10-year old John Milligen Seppings by enrolling him as a midshipmen in *Dunkirk*. In 1789 John went on to serve as midshipman in HMS *Penelope*, and then in the 98-gun HMS *Queen* aboard which he passed for lieutenant on 14 October 1793. For the next nine years he served in that rank in a variety of other ships ending with three years in the huge 104-gun HMS *Ville de Paris*. In 1802, at the instigation of Admiral Lord St. Vincent, he was appointed Comptroller of Revenue cutters, according to family reports rather against his will. He died in 1826. There is a stone memorial to him in Chudleigh Church, Devon, which reads: 'John Milligen Seppings Esq. Lieutenant R.N., for many years filling an important post in HM Customs. Died 23.3.1826. An only brother erected this Monument.' (That only brother was of course, our Robert, and indicates the regard that always existed between them.) One of the other midshipmen on board *Dunkirk* was 13-year old Peter Puget, who later sailed as a lieutenant with King's Lynn born Captain George Vancouver in HMS *Discovery* to the Pacific in 1791. Puget Sound, on which the city of Seattle now stands, was named after him. The greatest moment of Puget's career could have come in 1804 when he produced detailed plans for a fleet of fireships to be led by him in an attack on the port of Brest, a plan that was called off at a late hour. Instead, his greatest moment came during the Second Battle of Copenhagen in 1807, when the British advance squadron under his command sustained heavy fire from Danish shore batteries whilst supporting military units onshore. Peter Puget C.B., by then a rear admiral, died at Bath in 1822.

Captain Milligen and his wife Martha (née Phillips, 1732-1811) gave all the signs of being a very kindly couple. Already very well off as a beneficiary of his father's will, as a retired captain he would also have been superannuated on half-pay, and so it was he who began the family tradition of looking after less fortunate members of the family, a tradition to which our Robert Seppings paid far more than just lip-service over the course of time. The Milligen house in Plymouth was large enough to comfortably accommodate all his adopted relatives and Robert always held fond memories of his childhood there. In due course his sister Lydia returned home to help her mother in Fakenham, and his brother John Millgen Seppings, as we have seen, was at sea. Despite the break-up of his family Robert always held his birth mother in deep affection and she travelled to see him in Plymouth (and later to his homes in Chatham and London) quite regularly until she passed away at Fakenham in 1821.

The year 1782 must been an altogether busy one for Captain Milligen for late in it, and no doubt using more of the interest that was his to dispense, he arranged for Robert to be apprenticed to John Henslow, Master Shipwright at Plymouth Dockyard. Henslow would have interviewed the lad before accepting him and one can assume that Robert must have made a good impression. He was, in fact, a very lucky young man, for if any aspiring Royal Dockyard apprentice shipwright at that time could have chosen the Master Shipwright to whom to be apprenticed, it is likely he would have chosen Henslow who by that time had built up quite a reputation for himself. [5]

Born in 1730 Henslow was himself apprenticed in 1745 at Woolwich Dockyard to Sir Thomas Slade (1703-1771), the man who designed Nelson's HMS *Victory*. (Slade, who lies buried in St. Clement's churchyard in Ipswich, had

---

[5] The record of Seppings' indenture is to be found in the IR/1 series, 62, f181, National Archives, Kew.

been apprenticed to his uncle Benjamin Slade, one-time Master Shipwright at Plymouth Dockyard. It was Benjamin Slade who late in the1740s recommended one of his shipwrights 'into the service of the Honourable East India Company'. (That man was a certain Gabriel Snodgrass who will feature heavily later in this Seppings' story.)

Henslow was holding the post of quarterman (an intermediate rank between that of shipwright and foreman) in 1771 when the Navy Board sent him to survey the site of Buckler's Hard on the Beaulieu River where Henry Adams, the then private owner of that shipbuilding site where some of the navy's smaller ships had been constructed since about 1696, was seeking to expand in order to build larger vessels. The Navy Board had previously deemed this to be impractical but now Henslow recommended that four new slipways could be built, including one further upstream, that at 165 feet in length and angled towards a bend in the river to provide more room for launching, would be capable of building 64-gun vessels. His recommendations were accepted by the Board, a measure of the high regard in which he was held.[6] (In 1781, Nelson's favourite ship HMS *Agamemnon* of 64 guns entered the water from that new long slipway. It has been reported that when under the command of Nelson, that ship's decks resounded with Norfolk-sounding voices, for the great man born in Burnham Thorpe and who never lost his own accent, always did much of his recruiting in the county.)

On 15 February 1775 Henslow was made Master Shipwright at Plymouth and was there involved in overseeing the construction of such ships as HMS *Medusa* (50 guns), HMS *Anson* (64 guns), and HMS *Royal Sovereign*, a 100-gun vessel that one day would be the flagship of Vice Admiral Cuthbert Collingwood when he was second in command to Nelson at the Battle of Trafalgar. In 1784 Henslow was promoted to the post of Surveyor of the Navy, the Admiralty's chief designer of ships, a post he was to hold (either solely or conjointly with another remarkable shipbuilder called William Rule) until his retirement. He was knighted in 1793. In 1806 he retired to Sittingbourne in Kent where he died in September 1815. (His grandson John Steven Henslow was a well-known naturalist and a mentor of Charles Darwin.)
Young Robert Seppings had entered into an apprenticeship in the 'dark and ancient secret arts of the shipwright' – called that because in those days the

---

[6] Holland, *Buckler's Hard*.

rules of shipbuilding were still largely rule-of-thumb and passed down by word-of-mouth. The apprenticeship was to last for the standard seven-year period. (At age 15 Robert was a year older than the minimum allowable age that had been lowered to 14 by Navy Board Order in 1765.) In commercial shipyards the number of apprentices each Master could have was limited only by the needs of the business, but in the Royal Dockyards it was different because the Crown was paying the apprentices' wages. A Navy Board order dating from 1680 had fixed the maximum number of apprentices for each grade of Yard Officer, varying from five for the Master Shipwright, down to one for any 'deserving' shipwright who had recently completed his own training. As with all other trades, these apprenticeships were covered by documents called indentures, which had to be signed, sealed and delivered before a Magistrate or other official. (In a commercial yard a stamp duty had to be paid to make the indentures legally binding, but this did not apply in Royal yards.) In all cases, an upfront premium was paid to the Master by the apprentice's father (or other benefactor), the size of it reflecting the Master's reputation: in Henslow's case the premium would have been substantial and paid for by Captain Milligen. In 1819 Seppings himself wrote that his apprenticeship 'was at a considerable expense to his friends'.

By signing the indentures the apprentice agreed that his Master, and not himself, received the whole of his wages over the period of the indentures. Out of those sums the Master would grant the apprentice (or his father or benefactor if that was a condition of the indentures) a portion, usually up to about a third of the whole. Therefore, including the premium, the Master could make a great deal of money out of the system, whilst the apprentice could look forward to a career in shipbuilding and to one day having apprentices of his own out of which to make money. That is assuming that he passed out satisfactorily and had not during the period of his indentures blotted his copybook by fornicating, getting drunk, or getting married even! The part of the indenture covering behaviour, after pointing out that he 'must not contract marriage', went on, 'nor be guilty by word or action of any immoral, indecent, irregular, or improper conduct or behaviour in any respect whatsoever; but shall and will demean himself at all times with strict propriety and submission to his superiors'. (One might conclude that the result of all that was a quick and permanent goodbye to any sort of normal youth-hood behaviour.)

It seems that whenever the exigencies of the service allowed him to be away from the dockyard, young Robert spent time back in the Milligen home which was not too far away, for as we have seen, it was reported that his upbringing in that household was a happy one.[7] One can assume, therefore, that the strict working conditions in the yard were somewhat alleviated by the non-working part of his life. (During those home breaks it is more than possible that the Milligens took the opportunity to improve Robert's basic education with extra tuition.)

Admiralty dockyard apprentices were divided by custom and practice into two distinct groups. The first and by a long way the smallest group, consisted of lads who were articled to shipyard officers and destined if they remained in the service, to one day become such yard officers themselves. The second group consisted of those articled to 'ordinary' shipwrights and so could never expect to rise higher than shipwright themselves. (According to James Haas, there was a further sub-division in that top group, for only those lads who had been apprenticed to an officer holding the rank of Master Shipwright, ever gained that exalted rank.[8]) However, as in other professions, all apprentices were expected to learn from the bottom up, and so all would have started out along the following lines.

A budding shipwright apprentice was required to learn something about every job in the dockyard by the method now known as training on the job. According to a list in Admiralty records dating from 1739 there were thirty-one categories of workmen in the Royal Dockyards, and young Robert would have worked alongside men engaged in most of them for varying periods of time. Almost certainly his training would have begun with the filthiest and, literally, the lowest-of-the-low jobs, that carried out by so-called scavelmen who were labourers particularly concerned with the cleaning out and pumping out of docks. He would have learned from caulkers how to use oakum and heated pitch for sealing the seams of deck planking, another dirty but essential task. He would have spent periods with such artificers as joiners, carpenters, sawyers, coopers, blockmakers and treenailmooters. (The latter made the treenails which were circular wooden pins used for securing the planks and timbers of ships.) Later on he would have learned about the many different types of timber used in shipbuilding

---

[7] Packard, *Sir Robert Seppings and the Timber Problem.*
[8] Haas, *A Management Odyssey: the Royal Dockyards, 1714-1914.* p. 22

and how best to treat and store them before use to aid longevity. He would have been taught how to select the best 'compass timbers', which are those parts of a tree which grow naturally curved and bent and were used in places like the turn of the bilge and the junctions between deck and side frames. No doubt trips into the local forests were included in the training so that he could see for himself how trees were selected for felling and how they were then sawn into usable sections. He almost certainly would have spent time working in a sawpit, including being the man in the pit at the lower end of the saw who was on the receiving end of a continuous shower of sawdust. He is likely to have enjoyed some short periods at sea, for dockyard employees sometimes attended a ship during her trials in case something went wrong, or to complete unfinished work.

After having imbibed the basics of his craft he would have been taught how ship-plans were drawn, and how the lines of the ship could then be chalked out full-size on the wooden floor of the Mould Loft, off which patterns could be 'lifted'. These Mould Lofts were said to hold so many of the shipwrights' secrets, that they were always well protected from prying eyes. One of the ships on which he possibly worked as an apprentice because his master John Henslow was the Master Shipwright involved in its construction, was the 100-gun HMS *Royal Sovereign*, already mentioned above.

At some stage Robert must have received tuition from someone highly skilled in carpentry, because during his apprenticeship he constructed several ship models that show exquisite workmanship. There are examples in the National Maritime Museum at Greenwich and others in London's Science Museum and in museums abroad.

At sometime during his apprenticeship he, together with other lads in the superior group, would have been taken directly under the wing of the Master Shipwright, who under the Surveyor based in London, was responsible for building all ships within his particular dockyard. Now, much time would be spent in such special places as the drawing office working alongside and learning from yard officers. The drawings attached to some of the papers Robert Seppings wrote about his inventions show that he had developed considerable skills in draughtsmanship. Furthermore, whatever the standard of education he had received back in Fakenham, by the end of his apprenticeship in 1789 he had developed a considerable skill in descriptive writing, as is shown in his official correspondence and papers. One also supposes that some management skills, those of the era and so very basic from the modern point of view, would have been learned at this stage.

Sadly, Captain Milligen did not live to see his adopted son's graduation in 1789 as he died in the previous year. However, by that time Robert had another patron to exercise career-enhancing interest on his behalf in the form of John Henslow who, even after being promoted to the London-based post of Surveyor of the Navy in 1784, would still have taken an interest in the training and progress of his apprentices, but from a distance. (Henslow had almost certainly however, had to get one of the other local shipwright officers to take direct charge of his apprentices and arrange for that officer to receive the apprentices' wages instead of himself.) Robert rose through the ranks of shipwright, quarterman and then foreman, and was appointed Assistant to the new Master Shipwright at Plymouth, Joseph Tucker, in 1797: the last two advancements seem to have been rapid ones for he had still been a quarterman when he married his first cousin Charlotte Milligen in Charles the Martyr Church, Plymouth in 1795. Almost certainly, Henslow's influence can be seen in that rate of progress. On taking up the post as Tucker's assistant, Robert Seppings and his family would have moved into the accommodation within the Dockyard that went with that position.

One can assume that the union of Robert aged 28, and Charlotte aged 21 (who was described by a contemporary observer as being pretty), was a love match between two people who had enjoyed each other's company and grown fond of each other during the thirteen years they had both been together in the Milligen household. The marriage could have helped his long-term career prospects too, as in 1788 Charlotte's older (by eight years) sister, Martha Phillips Milligen had married in Charles Church, Plymouth, Lieutenant (later Vice Admiral Sir) Richard Dacres and in the fullness of time their two sons became Admiral Sir Sidney Colpoys Dacres, and Field Marshall Sir Richard James Dacres. So, by his sister-in-law's (and cousin's) marriage to a Dacres, Robert had become connected to a remarkable dynasty that produced more than a handful of senior naval officers. The Charles the Martyr Church in Plymouth (severely damaged by bombs during WW2) became a sort of Seppings family church, for in 1804 Robert's brother John Milligen also married there. He married Ann Marshall Lockyer, and they produced a very large family as we shall see.

The marriage of Robert and Charlotte produced a total of ten children in a period covering only sixteen years. The first two were born at Plymouth before the turn of the century. Martha Milligen Seppings born in 1796 and John Milligen Seppings two years later; they were named after the couple's parents by adoption and both were baptised in the 'family church'. This particular John Milligen Seppings should not be confused with Robert's younger brother of exactly the same name; the son became one of his father's apprentices and was to follow in his footsteps although his talents were to take him far away from Britain to the Indian sub-continent. There will be a deal more said about him later in this book.

The records show that at Plymouth Robert took on the first two of his apprentices, John Palmer in 1797, and William J. Hayward in 1799.[9] However, he was to enjoy the benefit of pocketing their earnings for only a few years. By an Order in Council issued in May 1801, all Royal Dockyard officers were deprived of their apprentices' earnings with immediate effect, causing quite a reduction in their total emoluments. But that would not have concerned Robert for long, for very soon his career really took off and his prospects soared.

---

[9] IR 1 series, 68 f189 and 69 f122 respectively, National Archive.

2
At Plymouth Dockyard: The Beginnings of Invention, and of Controversy

When he was appointed Joseph Tucker's assistant, Robert Seppings became one of the Royal Plymouth Yard's management team. From now on he was expected to look at labour relations from the perspective of a senior manager. The Navy Board in London administered all the Royal Dockyards through a chain of Commissioners one of whom was resident at each yard, and all yards were expected to follow the general administrative guidelines set by the Board including all matters concerning employment. The Board could and did, mulct pay as a punishment for any minor infringement of its rules, but its principle sanction was discharging men from its employ. However, in the wartime conditions prevailing at this time, the Board's over-riding responsibility was to keep the yards working so that main sanction was, in general, only used sparingly.

The Navy Board expected its labour force workers to make any complaints in the form of petitions, and ones most humbly phrased at that. Because most basic dockyard salaries had remained at a constant level since the 1690s, and as wartime inflation had raised prices generally and recent harvest failures had increased the price of bread particularly, and, added to all that the fact that wages were by custom always paid quarterly in arrears, there was quite a lot for the dockyard men to complain about. In consequence there were many petitions. Royal Dockyard historian Philip MacDougall once wrote, 'Whereas the strike, or threat of similar forms of action, was nothing less than a demand, the submissively presented petition was a formalized request couched in highly deferential language. This maintained the accepted relationship between employer and employee, while giving time for a considered answer'.[10] The trouble with that approach was, leaving aside the large element of paternalism involved, that it tended to take a long time. In fact, according to R.A. Morriss, the Board had paid no attention

---

[10] See MacDougall's article in Lunn and Day, eds. *History of Work & Labour in the Royal Dockyards.*

at all to any of the petitions it had received during the twelve months ending in the Spring of 1801.[11]

It was at Plymouth in 1800 just as the labour relations situation began to heat up, that Assistant Master Shipwright Robert Seppings, then responsible for work carried out on ships in the naval dry-dock there, first came to public notice when he invented a method whereby the area around the keel of a ship in dry-dock could much more easily than theretofore be made available for inspection and repair. Under the previous system, after the water had been pumped from the dry-dock, in order to examine and make repairs to the keel area an army of men (up to 500 for a large sized ship) had been required to lift the ship with the aid of tackles associated with sets of tall sheer-legs backed up by hand-operated cranes, off the wooden blocks upon which she had been settled.

An article by Alexander Tilloch appeared in the *Philosophical Magazine* in 1805, describing *Mr. Seppings' Method of Obviating the Necessity of Lifting Ships*, and telling how the invention had come about. In September 1800, whilst in charge of dry-docking the huge 114-gun 1st Rate HMS *San Josef* (a Spanish ship captured at the Battle of St. Vincent in 1797 and taken into the Royal Navy without a change of name), Seppings had taken particular note of the massive effort and length of time it took after the water had been pumped out of the dry-dock to lift her off the wooden blocks situated down the centreline of the dock. In a moment of imaginative genius it occurred to him that it should be possible to redesign the blocks so that the facility for removing them would be assisted by the ship's own weight. He experimented with models (using a hand-screw as a substitute for the weight of the ship) and came up with a three-wedge design of block, two of the wedges being arranged horizontally, and the other one vertically above the other two. (For the methodology used to remove the blocks, see below.) The experiment so impressed his superiors that he was given permission to experiment with the small 14-gun sloop HMS *Spitfire,* commanded by Commander (later Captain) Robert Keene (c.1763-1835). The three-wedge blocks used were cut from hardwood, and the best angle at which to cut them was found by trial-and-error. That ship experiment too, was a resounding success. Robert Seppings with his trial-and-error, rule-of-thumb methodology, had achieved something of which any professor in the field of applied mathematics would have been proud.

---

[11] Morriss, *Labour Relations in the Royal Dockyards, 1801-1805*, Mariner's Mirror, Vol. 82, 1976.

The next trial came with the docking of HMS *Canopus* in August 1801. (This vessel was a captured French 74-gun ship built at Toulon in 1794 as the *Le Franklin*, no doubt in honour of Benjamin Franklin who had been the American States' ambassador to France during the American War of Independence. As an interesting aside, Captain Francis Austen, brother of the novelist Jane Austen – a connection that enabled her to write knowledgably on naval matters in her books – commanded this ship in 1805.) Lessons learned during the *Spitfire* trial caused Seppings to have the vertical wedge of his system lined with half-inch wrought iron plate, whilst the two horizontal ones were now made of solid cast iron, and in addition, 'On the bottom of the dock, in the wake of each block, is a plate of iron ¾ inch thick so that the iron at all times acts in contact with iron'. (Present author's note: iron moving against iron involves much less friction than wood against wood, or wood against iron.)

The methodology used in the dry-docking operation was now as follows. Firstly, the ship was positioned to sit on the centre-line of blocks as the water in the dock was pumped out. Then, as the ship settled, sets of substantial shoring timbers were placed on either side at the turn-of-the-bilge level. With the ship seated on the new three-part blocks and safely shored, the two horizontally placed wedges of each block were then knocked out by repeated blows applied alternately from fore and then aft, by wheel-mounted battering-rams each manned by a handful of men, causing the ship's own weight, just as Seppings had theorised, to help press the wedges out. When the horizontal wedges were free, the vertical one fell to the floor of the dock, leaving the keel area free of all obstacles and safely sitting on the bilge shoring timbers. (Judicious placement of these bilge shores was critical so that they did not interfere with the working of the ramming operations. See diagram taken from Tilloch's article.) After the remedial work on the keel had been completed, the blocks were replaced by reversing the removal operation.

So, an operation that had previously required the efforts of up to 500 men could now be carried out by about 20. Not only that, 'the time to disengage each [block] is 1 – 3 minutes', a speed which meant that the entire operation of dry-docking and repairs, including any re-caulking required and then the subsequent undocking, could now be achieved 'on one spring tide'. (Present author's note: spring tides occur twice in a lunar month of 29 days. So 'one spring tide' was about a fortnight.)

Seppings' Blocks as they came to be called, had significantly reduced the direct costs of dry-docking, but there was much more to it than just that. During the three years from January 1798 to December 1800 for example, a total of 106 ships of various classes had been 'lifted' at Plymouth, and had Seppings system been available during that period, then 'that number could have been considerably increased', wrote Mr. Tilloch. In the long run, therefore, these much faster turn-round times meant that fewer ships were required in the fleet.

Tilloch reported:

> 'The invention may be applied with great advantage… to erect shores
> to support any great weights, as for instance, to prop up a building
> during the repair of its foundation etc. Captain Wells, of his Majesty's
> ship Glory, of 98 guns, used wedges of Mr. Seppings' invention, for a
> fid of a top-gallant mast of that ship…from repeated trials…the wedge
> fids have been found in every respect to answer the problem [of lifting
> out the top-mast] much more quickly than hitherto.'

He then went on:

> 'But it is Mr. Seppings' wish that that it should be understood that the
> idea of applying his invention [to that task] originated with Captain
> Wells, who well understood the principle, and had received from him
> a model of the invention.'

Captain (later Vice Admiral) Thomas Wells (1759-1811) was one of the pall-bearers at Nelson's funeral, positions reserved for men who had served with the great man. (Wells had been a fellow captain of Nelson in the Mediterranean Fleet at the Battle of Hyeres in July 1795. Both were in command of 64-gun ships, Wells in HMS *Defence*, Nelson in HMS *Agamemnon*.) Wells' grandson William was responsible for some of the drainage systems in The Fens. He later built a public house at Holme, near Peterborough in the 1850s called the *Admiral Wells*. It is still there and, as it is situated in the low-lying fens, it is officially recognized as the lowest pub in England.

Even the usually parsimonious Admiralty must have appreciated the size of the savings involved in using Seppings' Blocks, for in 1803 that body awarded him the then princely bonus of £1,000 for the invention. In that same year he was also awarded the Gold Medal of the Society of Arts. The kudos surrounding those awards were, however, marred for him by a claim made by Commander Keen of HMS *Spitfire*, who wrote to the Admiralty stating that the invention was his, and that he should, at the very least, share in any award. Although Keen's claim was given short shift and dismissed out of hand, the incident caused Seppings much distress. In a letter to the Admiralty he wrote:

> 'At this time it has particularly distressed my mind in consequence of the debilitated state of my body from an accident I received while attempting to dock the *Ruby*. I must confess I am at a loss to account for Captain Keen's treatment towards me, as I am not conscious of meriting such an aspersion from him or anyone else.'

It is clear that the Keen affair caused Seppings considerable annoyance and mortification. We shall see as we go along that this was not to be the last time that Robert Seppings was to suffer accusations of that sort; no, not by the longest of long chalks.

It is quite common for inventors to be regarded with jealously by others in their field, but on top of that there may have been other particular reasons why some of Seppings' shipyard colleagues began to look upon him with rather jaundiced eyes. The general statement can be made that dockyard jobs were always very much family oriented, with jobs mostly passed down from generation to generation as a sort of birthright. This passage of the baton down the family line did not, of course, always produce the most skilled workforce, but it did lead to a largely placid working environment and it also made recruitment easier. Only when authority attempted to change this hoary system – of such long-standing in the trade as to be considered almost as holy as apostolic succession – or try to import other 'improvements' into the ultra-conservative world of the dockyard, did fierce opposition arise. No documentary evidence has been found to confirm that the introduction of Seppings' Blocks with its concomitant reduction in staffing levels in dry-dock operations, made him unpopular with some of his fellows, but its effect on overall job opportunities was so vast, it must have.

The timing of the second experiment of his blocks on HMS *Canopus* with its obvious effect on future overall manpower requirements was perhaps not propitious. On 31 March 1801, only four months earlier, the dockyard artificers at Plymouth, disillusioned by the non-effect of their petitions, left the dockyard in 'a tumultuous manner' over the arrest of one of their number for being concerned in a 'riot' within the dock area. In April there were more artificer riots in Plymouth, and another at Sheerness that, although it appears to have been a disconnected affair, added to the Navy Board's overall problem.

At around the same time as the general introduction of his new blocks, there were two other well-documented factors that did effect employment in the dockyards and which would have served to mask any 'Seppings effect'. The first was the signing of the Treaty of Amiens in March 1802 that brought peace between Great Britain and France. Although that peace was to last only until Britain declared war again on 18 May 1803, that lull in the Napoleonic Wars eased the pressure on the dockyard force and caused the Admiralty, always under governmental pressure in peacetime to save tax-payer's money, to lay men off.

The second factor, however, had by far the greater effect. That was the appointment of Admiral John Jervis, Lord St. Vincent, to the post of First Lord of the Admiralty in February 1801. Famous as the victor of the battle from which he took his title and for raising the standards of discipline and efficiency in the British Mediterranean fleet to the degree that made that victory possible, 'Old Jervie' as he was called behind his back, was a particularly harsh disciplinarian and a man whose experience in labour relations lay solely in a strict interpretation of the disciplinary rules enshrined in the Royal Navy Articles of War of 1757. In that document just about any offence on board ship could result in an offender either being hanged at the yardarm or receiving a multiple-lash sentence. Through age and ill-health, by the time of his new appointment he had degenerated into an unreasonable tyrant who used severity in discipline merely, it seems, because he had the power to do so. On top of that, Jervis seems always to have held the Navy Board, one of whose tasks was to run the dockyards, in low regard and had a particularly poor opinion of so-called 'dockyard mateys' including shipwrights. He was convinced (not without some justification it must be said) that the Navy Board and the dockyards were infested with idle people out to make a fast buck, and so hoped to be, to use his own words, 'of some use in stopping, if not radically reforming, the flagrant abuses which pervade the naval service, both civil and military'. (A traditional navy question-and-answer joke persists to this very day: Q. *How many dockyard mateys work in Portsmouth?* A. *About half of them!*)

Some of the abuses by personnel that Jervis attempted to reform had been so systemised over decades or even centuries, that they were considered standard perks of the job, and went to make up for low and late-paid wages. One of them was the shipwrights' right to take home for firewood so-called 'chips', the bits that flew off wood as it was shaped with an adze. Over the passage of time these carried-home 'chips' had grown larger and larger until it was accepted that any piece of wood qualified, provided it did not exceed six feet in length (perhaps not coincidently, the length of the nautical fathom), which meant that a lot of timber was being marched out of the dockyard gates at the end of each shift. It was reported that most of the buildings in the workers' settlements that developed outside the lines of Sheerness Dockyard, and other places, showed a remarkable degree of similarity in construction especially in the use of short boards; not only that, there was also a remarkable sameness in the decoration of these buildings as dockyard paint was disappearing in the same way. It was not only at shift-end times when this was a problem. Women were allowed into the dockyard carrying their men's breakfasts, and they too were walking out with their baskets full of chips and sometimes with nails and pieces of iron tucked under their skirts. And as if all that was not enough, so-called receivers had taken up residence in some of the houses close to dockyards, men who had funds to pay for any purloined materials. An example of how even large items were sometimes smuggled out was when a coil of rope (of the standard 600 fathoms in length and so pretty bulky) produced in the Chatham Rope Shed one morning, was discovered in a house outside in the afternoon of the same day.[12]

Had Admiral Jervis gone about the tasks of making changes in personnel and abolishing perks and stopping theft and pilfering, with even a small degree of tact, moderation and diplomacy, instead of diving into this man-management nightmare wielding a monday-hammer (the shipyard name for a sledge-hammer and called that because it always seemed easier to wield on the first day of the working week), he could have carried the approval of many good men with him and, probably, been considerably more successful. As it was, some of his hastily made decisions, like the 'easy solution' of sacking men for instance, were highly damaging to the institutions he was attempting to reform. According to House of Commons papers, one result of his tactics was that in the first two years of his three-year reign, there was a reduction of about 1,400 skilled men in dockyard employment, 940 of them from Portsmouth and Plymouth alone, and many of them had nothing at all to

---

[12] For an excellent summary of pilfering and theft from the dockyards, see the article on the subject by R.J.B. Knight, in Mariner's Mirror, Vol.61, 1975, No.3.

do with the customary reduction of men caused by the short-lived period of peace that came in the middle of his period in office. Lord St. Vincent could not bear to be crossed, so included in those who lost their jobs were 340 men who had helped to organize petitions over an increase in basic wages, 'or had a reputation for being recalcitrant'. All that resulted in a critical manpower shortage when the war resumed in May 1803. That reduction in manpower had a side-effect; it took a great deal of the heat out of the artificers' demands for more money and even more heat was taken out when the Board agreed that a proportion of the quarterly wage payment could be paid out weekly. (It was called subsistence money.) With all that going on, it is of little wonder that another side-effect, the one we have called the Seppings effect, was hidden from everyone, except one supposes from those directly effected by it.

A friendship that was to last for life began at Plymouth around 1799 between Robert Seppings and Joseph Whidbey. Whidbey (1755-1833) was one of that great band of Masters R.N. who down the years were the navy's navigators and ship-handlers. (Early in his naval career, the explorer Captain James Cook held that warrant rank before becoming a commissioned officer; and one of several Norfolkmen to hold it was John Fryer of Wells, who in 1787 sailed as master and second-in-command of HMS *Bounty* under Lieutenant William Bligh, and who in 1789 was the only member of the crew to make any attempt to stop the now famous mutiny that took place on board. It is possible that Fryer and Whidbey were acquainted because their professional paths crossed several times.)

Whidbey had sailed as Master with Captain George Vancouver in HMS *Discovery* on his voyage of discovery to the Pacific between 1791-5, and his navigational and cartographic skills had come to the attention of Admiral Lord St. Vincent who, in 1799, commissioned him to survey Torbay, an important naval anchorage on the Channel coast. It was during the months of that survey, that the Seppings/ Whidbey friendship developed. Then in 1806 the Admiralty commissioned the famous engineer John Rennie to carry out a feasibility study on the construction of a protective breakwater in Plymouth Sound, and Rennie took Whidbey, who was then Master Attendant at Woolwich, with him to advise on hydrographic matters. Work on the now world-renowned Plymouth Breakwater, one of the largest engineering works conducted in 19th century Britain, began in 1811. It was built to Rennie's design although the work was superintended throughout by Whidbey who moved to Plymouth for the purpose. From his house there was a splendid view of the work as it went on, and during the summer of 1814 Robert Seppings paid him a visit and 'saw and admired the growing structure'.

Correspondence between Whidbey and Rennie suggests that Whidbey had retained a sailor's salty sense of humour. When a local dignitary, Sir Francis Northwell, persistently pestered the pair with the idea that a large hole in the bottom of Plymouth Harbour might complicate construction, Whidbey wrote that should such a feature be discovered, it should be named *Lady Northwell's Hole*.

Whidbey, retired to Taunton in Somerset, and it is perhaps a measure of the closeness of their relationship that when the time came, Seppings did the same. It is of interest that the *Taunton Courier* of 8 January 1833 reported that Whidbey had attended a Masonic Dinner in the town, and that he had 'carried with him his Masonic Certificate twice round the world'. Perhaps Seppings joined the same Lodge, for many men of industry at that time were Freemasons.

Seppings must have kept himself very busy at Plymouth for, at around the same time that he invented his system of dry-dock blocks, he also took the first steps in developing his ideas on strengthening the structures of wooden ships. A problem that had plagued shipbuilders since the misty beginnings of the industry, was that the wooden structure suffered continually from deflection in a seaway caused by ever changing forces of weight and buoyancy as the ship passed through the waves. (The main stresses involved are technically known as compression and tension.) They caused the hull to alternate between a condition known as 'hogging', when the central section of the ship is buoyed up and the bow and stern sections forced down, and then, when the converse happened, the condition known as 'sagging', when the central part is forced down compared to the extremes. These continuous changes from compression to tension created deflections in the side frames – ribs if you like – and caused the ship's hull planking to open up and the caulking between them to be disturbed which resulted in water getting in and timbers rotting, so further weakening the hull. (Newly constructed ships often had a built in hog from the start due to mal-construction techniques, which aggravated the situation.)

The first experiment of his strengthening system was the partial introduction of it during the repairs to HMS *Glenmore* at Plymouth in 1800. This information comes from an article included as an *Appendix* to the 1822 revised edition of David Steel's book on naval architecture (originally published in 1794).[13] The revision of the book, which in many respects was a re-write, was carried out at the publisher's request by John Knowles, and it was he who wrote an appended 60-page article to that work entitled *Principles & Practices of Constructing the Royal & Mercantile Navies invented by Sir Robert Seppings.* Knowles wrote in that Appendix, 'As all arts and sciences have their infancy and gradually advance to maturity… [Seppings, plan began with] partial introductions of the system… [when he] laid some planks in *Glenmore*'s hold crossing the footwalling in a diagonal direction, in order that they might act as ties to strengthen the ship.' Knowles went on, 'the success that attended this experiment induced Seppings to extend the system'. In fact the extension of the system took place over several years as we shall see in the next chapter.

(The *Glenmore* had been built in 1759 as the *Tweed.* In the latter half of the 18th century a number of frigates were constructed largely from fir, known as an 'inferior' timber as it had no great longevity, because of the shortage of 'superior' timbers, like oak and elm. The vessels involved, were mostly in the *Tweed*, *Unicorn*, and *Pallas* classes, and were known as 'fir frigates' and were considered to be of questionable value.[14] Built of light-weight timber they were fast sailers, but that was their only redeeming characteristic. Seamen disliked serving in them as their fir hulls shattered easily, with dangerous splinters flying everywhere, when struck by a cannon shot.)

John Knowles, the eldest son of a shipwright of the same name and his wife May, was born at Deptford in 1781. His father worked in the Royal Dockyard at that place. No doubt young John began some form of training under his father at an early age and must have shown great promise, as from around the turn of the century (at about the same time as the *Glenmore* experiment) he was appointed clerk in the Surveyor's Office of the Navy Board when the

---

[13] Steel, The Elements and Practice of Naval Architecture.
[14] See the MA thesis of Peter Erik Flynn entitled *HMS Pallas: Historical Reconstruction of an 18th C. Royal Navy frigate.*

surveyor was Sir William Rule. Knowles' advancement was rapid, for he was promoted to Chief Clerk in about 1806 and held that post continually for twenty-six years. That included the entire period of Robert Seppings' period as Surveyor, during which the pair became fast friends. It is likely then, that for over thirty years just about every document produced in that office, passed through his hands, which makes him a very reliable commentator.[15]

On the Seppings' family front, the first year of the new century brought another blessing, but one soon followed by tragedy. Mrs. Charlotte Seppings was delivered of her third child (and second daughter) in 1800 who was baptised Mary Milligen in Charles Church, Plymouth. Then in 1801, came the birth of a second son. Born on 31 August he was christened Robert Nankivel – the latter being the Cornish word for 'valley of the woodcock' – who was baptised on 7 October. He died in 1802.

This was an age when large families were commonplace. So were infant mortalities. Nevertheless, in view of Richard's early demise and other family tragedies yet to be related, it seems proper to mention the possibility that the consanguineous marriage of first cousins Robert and Charlotte might have been a factor in those events. Marriages between first cousins were lawful in Britain and allowed by the Church of England, but there has always been some prejudice against them (the marriage of Queen Victoria and Prince Albert notwithstanding), because of a perceived danger of passing on heredity diseases.[16] This prejudice may have been compounded by the rather ambivalent attitude of the Roman Catholic Church over this matter, which was officially to be against such marriages and yet allowed them to be contracted on payment for a dispensation.

---

[15] That he was very learned was proven by the fact that he was chosen to edit and revise Steel's book, the standard work on shipbuilding in Britain at that time. He went on to write a treatise under the long title, *An Inquiry into the Means which have been taken to Preserve the British Navy from the Earliest Period to the Present Time, from the Species of Decay, now denominated as Dry-Rot.* For that work he was made a Fellow of the Royal Society, and received gifts from European Royalty. He resigned from his post in 1832 when his salary was £650 per annum, a considerable one in those days. He is perhaps best remembered nowadays as the biographer in 3 volumes of his friend, the painter Henry Fuseli (1741-1825). At one time Knowles was a director of the Economic Life Assurance Company at Blackfriars. He died at Asburton in Devon in 1841. One can assume he had lived rather well, as when a few months after his demise the contents of his house came up for sale, the lots included over 100 dozen bottles of fine wines.

[16] It is, however, still illegal in some other countries and in about half of the states that comprise the United States.

3
Master Shipwright, Chatham Dockyard

In late 1803 Robert Seppings was promoted to the post of Master Shipwright at Chatham the largest of all the naval dockyards, and at that time almost certainly the largest industrial complex of any kind in the world. At 36, he was comparatively young for the post which proves that even an organization like the megalithic and sometimes hidebound Admiralty (known throughout the land as 'The Tree' because its roots and branches spread into just about every aspect of public life), could act promptly when they saw a rare talent and were prepared, just as they were with sea-going appointments (the rise of Nelson is an example), to override the general principle that promotion was based largely on seniority and patronage rather than on ability. This promotion almost certainly increased the hostility towards him in certain quarters, especially from any person senior to him in the service who may have considered himself overlooked.

At Chatham Dockyard he and his family took up residence in the largest of the houses that formed the four-floored and west-facing Officers' Terrace, each one of which had its own walled garden. (That terrace of houses is still there and now provides high-quality private accommodation.) He was living on the job as the saying goes, for his house was sited within only a short distance of all the main dockyard activities. That meant he and his family were surrounded as in every dockyard, by movement, noise and industrial fumes and smells: however, no doubt Charlotte and the youngsters had become used to that whilst living in similar though less spacious accommodation at Plymouth.

One of the first family matters he had to attend to at Chatham was the baptism of a daughter born soon after his arrival there. She was christened Charlotte Lucy, on 4 September 1803. Charlotte, no doubt named for her mother, was to have only a short life for she died when not yet six years old in June 1809 and was buried on the 30th of that month in St. Mary Churchyard, Chatham.

Robert Seppings' period in charge at Chatham was to prove highly successful. In contrast his family life was a mixture of happiness and great heartache, for Charlotte Lucy's early demise was not the only tragedy to be borne. In the Spring of 1806 another son, christened Andrew Sanders on 28 May, came along. In comparison with the other Seppings' offspring who survived into adulthood, very little is known about Andrew. The information that does exist indicates he was born an invalid of some kind, remained so for the rest of his life and never married. In Robert's will, proved in 1840, he left the Trustees £5,000 for Andrew's benefit, saying: "his state of mind being such as to render him unfit to manage his own affairs". It would seem that the Trustees took that duty seriously, for in the 1841 Census (the first one to give more information than a mere head-count), he is listed as a man of independent means lodging at Middle Row, St. Michael, Pembroke, with a surgeon called James Bryant and his family. He was then 35. When Andrew died in 1849 aged 43, he was still living at that address. One can safely surmise that his lodgement with a professional medical man was no accident.

The year after Andrew's birth brought a double tragedy. In August 1807 Charlotte Seppings was delivered of twins, Lydia Milligen and Robert Richard. They were baptised together on the 12th of that month and were buried together only a fortnight later in St. Mary Churchyard.

Happily the next two children were to outlive their parents. Louisa was born early in January 1811 and christened on the 16th. Helen Milligen, the last-born of the family, was born in November 1812 and christened on the 2nd of the following month. (Both married and had issue as we shall see.) According to the Packard papers, whilst he was serving at Chatham, Seppings often had his mother down from Norfolk to stay, a journey much shorter and so less arduous than those she had made to Plymouth. Packard went on to write,

> 'a pencil sketch of her on one such visit, drawn by one of the shipwrights circa 1810 when she was about 70, shows her with a firm happy expression, wearing glasses and sitting upright in a high-backed wooden chair with a frilly lace cap on her head and a woollen shawl round her shoulders, concentrating on her knitting cast on three needles.'

(That pencil sketch, reproduced in this book, suggests that the prominent and distinguished nose found in the portraits of Sir Robert and other members of his family, also reproduced here, was a Milligen rather than a Seppings feature.)

On arriving at Chatham the new Master Shipwright inherited the superintendence of at least two uncompleted ships from his predecessor. They were the 90-gun *Impregnable* and the 74-gun *Revenge*. The first ship in that dockyard to be superintended by him from scratch was the 36-gun frigate HMS *Meleager* whose keel was laid in June 1804. (Later, he was in charge of the construction of two of that ship's sisters, the *Iphigenia* and the *Orlando*.) He was also master shipwright in the construction of HMS *Warspite*, 74, the fourth in a line of seven naval ships to carry that proud name (which range from a 17th century galleon to a nuclear submarine).[17]

During his time at Chatham, Seppings received official plaudits for designing a new method for the long-term mooring of ships and also for a screw system that replaced the earlier tackle system used in loading and unloading lighters and barges. These show that his innovative genius was not strictly confined to shipbuilding and ship-repairing matters. There were others in this category. He designed (in 1803) iron cylinders for smoothing out copper sheets removed from one ship for re-use in another; a machine for making improved copper bolts (1807); an apparatus for comparing the strength and weight of ships' timbers (1812), and in that same year and in conjunction with Ferdinand Hicks, the yard's ironsmith, a new method of making anchors. His always active and penetrating gaze fell on the smallest of matters, and perhaps that was best illustrated when, by then well in to his period as Surveyor of the Navy, he devised a new method of preparing oakum for caulking in 1820. But they were all of small import when compared with some of his other achievements. His genius for invention and innovation, together with his reputation grew apace: unfortunately, as his inventions came along (some of which should more correctly be described as improvements on someone else's methodology), and spurred on perhaps by jealousy caused by his accelerated promotion, more accusations of plagiarism came along too.

We shall first discuss his system of strengthening the structure of ships with diagonal trussing between the frames of the traditional longitudinal arrangement. His system was first experimented with in the *Glenmore* in 1800. He compared it with the diagonal strengthening of the five-barred farmyard gates he remembered from his youth in Norfolk, some of which he must have passed time and time again on that mule route between Fakenham and Wells. Without those diagonals, he explained, those gates would soon have collapsed.

---

[17] Extrapolated from Winfield, *British Warships in the Age of Sail.*

John Knowles in his *Appendix* referred to in the previous chapter had gone
on to write,

> 'When the diagonal mode of shipbuilding was first brought forward
> to public notice, it was pronounced by some to be "without sense
> or science", while others , either from envy or an inaptitude to bring
> their minds to examine new combinations, predicted no less than
> the loss of ships that might be built thereby, if they proceeded to sea'.

Those criticisms, together with the Admiralty's usual tardiness in adopting
change, were probably the cause of the five-year delay before Seppings was
permitted to experiment again, with an improved system of his diagonal
trussing. This took place at Chatham in 1805, and this is how Knowles
described it in his work of 1822.

> 'When the *Kent* of 74 guns, a ship of large dimensions, was docked for
> repair at Chatham [between May and November 1805], it was found
> that she was in a general state of weakness, for an alteration had taken
> place from her original sheer…[having] arched no less than seventeen
> inches. [She had been launched at Woolwich in 1798.]'

As a partial remedy Robert Seppings, 'placed between the bends of vertical
riders already in the hold, diagonal ones lying at an angle of forty-five
degrees; and abutting against them and the original riders, trusses, at the
same angle in an opposite direction', wrote Knowles. He went on, 'this was
found in a great measure to preserve the sheer of the ship… this was an
approximation to the perfection of the plan as practised on the *Tremendous*
and which has been followed with slender modifications, from the year
1810'.

In fact, as usual when change came along, it did not go quite as easily as
that indicates. Although the system installed in the *Kent*, was also considered
a success by the Admiralty, there were still many doubters. According to
Knowles in a footnote to his work, this caused Charles Yorke, the new First
Lord of the Admiralty, a politician with little knowledge of the sea and ships,
in 1810 to instruct Sir James Barrow, Second Secretary, the navy's senior
civil servant, to set up a 'Committee of the most celebrated mathematicians
and naval and civil architects in the country for the examination of the system,
and it was from the favourable opinion given by them that this method was

adopted'.[18] One of the mathematicians involved, a man called Young, based his support on something he called 'fluxions' which were considered almost incomprehensible by other members of the committee. Of much greater moment perhaps, was that on the other side of the Channel, Napoleon Bonaparte, upon hearing of the meeting and who was desperately trying to raise the French Navy to the standard and size of the Royal Navy, commissioned the brilliant young French naval engineer and mathematician Charles Dupin to make a similar study. He too, came out in support of the Briton's methodology, but in a much clearer way.

The outcome was that Seppings' system, designed to prevent deflections from the regular state by strengthening the structure longitudinally with diagonal trusses, was used in full in the reconstruction of the 74-gun HMS *Tremendous* that took place at Chatham and was completed in January 1811. Measurements taken aboard *Tremendous* after her reconstruction showed that deflections to her hull in a seaway were now negligible. Seppings not only attended the measuring operations aboard the ship out in the North Sea, but it seems he also devised some of the measuring procedures used. After that the system was followed throughout the navy. During the 'Large Repair' to the *Albion*, for example, between 1810 and 1813, which was virtually a rebuild, the complete system was installed in her too and that ship lived on until 1836 when she was broken up at Deptford. (In *Tremendous* the diagonal riders were made from thick iron, an extra innovation that was generally adopted after 1813.)

But most of that (and the associated controversies involved) was in the future. For now, we return to the year 1806 and to what was possibly one of the most memorable of Seppings' early tasks at Chatham, that concerning the repairs to HMS *Victory*.

On 15 October 1805 the Battle of Trafalgar was fought and won. During the battle the flagship *Victory* was very badly mauled and the crew suffered 57 deaths, including that of Vice Admiral Lord Nelson, and 101 wounded. After emergency repairs at Gibraltar and sailing under a jury rig, the ship carrying the admiral's body limped home to arrive at Portsmouth on 4 December. (Amongst the many ships in the harbour there, all appropriately rigged and

---

[18] John Barrow was a great admirer of Seppings and his work. The two men had much in common, for Barrow a lad from a poor family in Lancashire, had also risen far up the ranks of society.

manned in honour of the arrival home of Britain's dead hero, was HM Storeship *Abundance* commanded by John Fryer of Wells-next-the Sea, who noted the event in his logbook.[19])

An initial survey of the ship's damage was carried out by shipwrights at Portsmouth Dockyard, accompanied by some of the ship's officers. One of the midshipmen concerned was Richard Roberts, and it is from his Journal that we get the following stark summary presented exactly as he wrote it.

'*Defects to HMS Victory 5th December 1805. Thos. M. Hardy Esq, Captain.*
The hull is much damaged by shot in a number of different places, particularly in the wales, strings, and spurketing, and some between wind and water. Several beams, knees and riders, shot through and broke; the starboard cathead shot away; the rails and timbers of the head and stem cut by shot; several of the ports damaged, and port timbers cut off; the channels and chainplates damaged by shot and the falling of the mizzen mast; the principle part of the bulkheads, halfports, and portsashes thrown overboard in clearing ship for action.

The mizzen mast shot away about 9 feet above the deck; the main mast shot through and sprung; the main yard gone; the main topmast and cap shot in different places; the main topsail yard shot away; the foremast shot through in a number of different places, and is at present supported by a topmast, and part of the topsail and crossjack yards; the fore yard shot away; the bowsprit jibboom and cap shot away, and the spritsail and spritsail topsail yards, and flying jibboom gone; the fore and main tops damaged; the whole of the spare topmast yards, hand-mast and fishes shot in different places, and converted into jury gear.'

The young midshipman ended his summary with the words, 'The ship makes in bad weather 12 inches of water an hour'.

Midshipman Richard Francis Roberts was born at Bridport, and the *Victory* which he joined in 1804, was his first ship. The vessel carried 22 midshipman and maybe the fact that two of his fellows had been killed and four others badly wounded in the battle, plus the nature

---

[19] See Fryer's *Abundance* logbooks in ADM52, National Archives, Kew

of the many damages he listed in his summary, was all too much for this young lad who was only in his very early teens, because it turned out that *Victory* was also his last ship. He left the service in 1806. We know something about one of his badly wounded comrades, who was also very young – Nelson in his letters referred to him as 'boy Rivers'. Midshipmen William Rivers' leg was amputated after he was struck by a flying fragment of timber caused by cannon shot. (A very high proportion of all battle injuries at this time were caused by such splinters.) For this wound Rivers was awarded an annual sum of £91-5s. from the Patriotic Fund. Despite his incapacity he was promoted lieutenant after passing the necessary examination in 1806. Lieut. Rivers apparently stayed on the books until 1824 when he took a shoreside appointment with the navy, and was amongst the still living survivors from Trafalgar who in 1847 were belatedly awarded the Naval General Service Medal and clasp. Rivers died at Greenwich Hospital in 1856, of which he had been Lieutenant-in-charge for 30 years. He was married, for it is recorded that his son, N.E. Rivers, was an aged resident in 1922 of the well-known charitable organisation called Morden College at Blackheath.

After a brief stay at Portsmouth, the *Victory* sailed for Chatham from whence Nelson's body was conveyed to Greenwich Hospital where it was to lay in state. The ship was then paid off and handed over to Master Shipwright Robert Seppings who conducted a more thorough survey of the damage. Then, on 6 March 1806 the ship was warped into No. 2 Dock. *The London Globe* in reporting this event said: 'It is a little remarkable that this beautiful ship should at this time be repairing in the very dock in which she was built, one and forty years ago'. According to Seppings, the docking was a cleverly managed job. In his report to the Navy Board he noted: 'I can find no ship that has been docked here that has drawn more water than the *Victory*, her draught being 19ft. 2 ins. abaft. The water in the dock on the day was 18ft.: on the slide 16ft. 9ins. (It being 1ft. 3ins. above the bottom of the dock.) Of course, the ship shewed [sic] abaft 2ft. 5ins. and about 2 ft. forward. She came in very well…eighteen feet is the height of a fair tide.'

The total repair work on the ship, which was completed on 4 May, cost £9,936. Although the work had been ordered expedited, for some reason unexplained in the records, she was then laid up at a time when the navy was suffering an acute shortage of ships. She lay 'in ordinary', which entailed being moored in a safe place with all her gear taken out including the masts, and being manned only with a skeleton crew. *Victory* remained in ordinary until March 1807. After that she saw more sea service interspersed with more periods in ordinary before finally ending her long sea-going career in 1812 when she entered Harbour Service.

> In Britain it has become traditional to believe that the Battle of Trafalgar fought on 21 October 1805 was so decisive a defeat for the French that, in one fell Nelsonian swoop it put paid to Napoleon's plans to invade Britain and also to any pretensions the French had of wresting supremacy of the sea away from the Royal Navy.
>
> Even in the narrow sense of ship losses, the battle cannot be considered a knock-out blow because, of the 33 ships-of-the-line in the Combined Franco/Spanish fleet, no less than 15, that is, close to half, managed to escape. In the wider sense Trafalgar was not decisive at all. After that battle France and her Allies still had many ships-of-the-line available and on top of that, Napoleon began building many more. All over the world there were many sea battles to come, and the threat of invasion to the British Isles did not disappear until 1810. Trafalgar certainly dented Napoleon's pride but it did nothing to affect his actions and aspirations on Continental Europe. (Only six weeks after Trafalgar, Napoleon's army gained what was arguably the most brilliant of all his victories at the Battle of Austerlitz against the combined Russian and Austrian armies.)
>
> So, after 1805, the fight for supremacy at sea went on, which meant that the shipbuilding facilities of both nations continued working at full pelt.

The battle damage Seppings noted aboard *Victory* in 1806 and the information he received about the large number of wood-splinter casualties the ship had sustained when under raking fire from the enemy, caused him to design a more rounded and stronger bow section which was eventually incorporated into the design of all new ships. (Note: 'To rake', was the operation of manoeuvring a ship into position so that her broadsides could be fired down the length of the adversary's gun decks.) From then on, the old-style comparatively flimsy beak-head arrangement was out and the rounded, stronger built-up bow section was in. Possibly the first ship to have a Seppings' built-up bow incorporated into its construction was the 120-gun HMS *Caledonia* launched in 1808, the original plans for this ship being altered for the purpose.

This new bow design after it became commonplace throughout the fleet, must have saved many lives. J. Fincham wrote the following in his authoritative *History of Naval Architecture* published in 1851.

> Previous to the introduction of Sir Robert Seppings' alterations, the bow was straight across at the cat-head, so low as to be in line with the upper deck port-sill and was boarded across with thin boarding and stanchions. But as this was not sufficient to resist even grape-shot, the crew were much exposed to the raking fire of the enemy, for it was observed in the *Victory* after the Battle of Trafalgar that while in many cases the largest shot had not gone through the round and solid part of the bow, the grape-shot had passed through this planking.

At around this same time Sepping's began introducing a more circular and stronger stern section too, because ships could be raked from the stern as well as from the bow, although that was not the only reason for this particular change. The wide, square stern of yore, often splendidly decorated with so-called 'gingerbread', not only presented a wonderful target for the foe, but the captain's and officers' quarters behind it did not provide much space for guns to be mounted, and restricted the angles of fire of those that were. Because the final version of this more circular, pinched-in stern section, somewhat resembled the rear end of a duck, seamen, who always know how to coin a coarse but fitting word or two, dubbed it a 'duck's arse'. During the major refit at Plymouth in 1814-15 of the *Caledonia* mentioned above, her stern was rebuilt to Seppings' new pattern. There is a model of this ship depicting the change in the National Maritime Museum, Greenwich.

HMS *Caledonia* was commanded by Captain Francis Austen, the novelist's brother, from 1810 to 1812, except for a brief period of a month when she was under the temporary command of Captain Peter Heywood. Heywood had been a midshipman in HMS *Bounty* at the time of the mutiny aboard that ship. Later, having been captured and arrested at Tahiti, he was tried at Portsmouth as a mutineer and was condemned to death. He was subsequently pardoned by King George and returned to his career in the navy.

Seppings' design change to the stern section of ships led to a charge of plagiarism, the one mentioned in the Foreword of this book, of which Sir John Barrow had written that Seppings was accused of pilfering it from the Dutch. We shall have more to say about this Dutch connection in the next chapter.

4
Surveyor of the Royal Navy

Strengthening ships with diagonal trusses in the longitudinal plane turned out to be by far the most important of Seppings' inventions, and its success must certainly have been a consideration when the Admiralty promoted him to the post of Surveyor of the Navy by letter-patent dated 14 June 1813. At the time of that promotion he was superintending the building of the *Howe* of 120-guns, the *Minotaur* and *Hercules*, both 74's, and the *Lively* frigate of 36-guns. According to naval historian David K. Brown, HMS *Howe* 'was probably the first *new* ship designed using Seppings fully developed scheme'.[20] (Although his 'scheme' was used, this ship was not one of his designs.) After Seppings' promotion, the completion of those four vessels fell to George Parkins, the new Master Shipwright at Chatham.

At the same time as Seppings' appointment, Joseph Tucker, the Master Shipwright at Plymouth where he had earlier been Seppings' superior, was conjointly raised to Surveyor – a double appointment device often resorted to during critical times when the duties involved were particularly arduous. Although Tucker was to hold that appointment until his death in 1831, little is known about him. He was appointed one of the Commissioners at Antwerp in 1814 where he was involved in examining captured enemy ships and deciding on their disposal along with the stores in the arsenal there. It is likely that from the start he was overshadowed by Seppings and in consequence slipped into a secondary role. Unlike Seppings and many others who held the title of Surveyor, Tucker was not knighted nor honoured in any other way. After Tucker's death, Seppings became the sole surveyor.[21]

We here relate what Seppings' himself said of his own appointment to the post of Surveyor in a Memorial he wrote to the Prince Regent, H.R.H. the Duke of Clarence on 1 March 1819. He wrote that he, 'sacrificed comfort

---

[20] DNB, 2nd edition, p. 766.

[21] According to the National Maritime Museum, Joseph Tucker is 'best remembered' as the designer in 1809 of a 170-gun ship with five decks of guns to be called the *Duke of Kent*. Perhaps the NMM had its corporate tongue in its cheek, for this monster in fact was never built. Tucker was the elder brother of Benjamin Tucker (1762-1829), once a naval purser who became Admiral Jervis's secretary, and briefly, a Second Secretary at the Admiralty.

and gained no emolument – as stated by the Select Committee of Finance, page 190 – by leaving the situation of Master Shipwright of Chatham dockyard and accepting that of Surveyor of His Majesty's navy, and which he was induced to do only from the consideration that he would be empowered thereby to protect those plans which he had brought forward, and to introduce others for the good of his Majesty's service'.[22] In other words, at the time of his appointment to the post, he did not receive an increase in salary above that which he had enjoyed at Chatham, despite the very significant increase in his responsibilities.

At the age of forty-six Robert Seppings had reached the apex of his profession. As Surveyor he was a member of the Navy Board, the body responsible for the supply and administration of the navy and its shore installations, and was one of its Commissioners. Until 1832 when the two were merged, this Board – sometimes alternatively referred to as the Navy Office – ran in parallel to the Board of Admiralty, which had overall operational control of the navy.[23] Since 1789 the Board's headquarters had been in the palatial edifice off the Strand called Somerset House, and the Surveyor had offices there and family accommodation.

The Surveyor's main duties as officially laid down, 'were to direct the preparations of drawings for all the ships and vessels ordered to be built for His Majesty's service, and to survey or examine the Reports of all surveys taken of the hulls, masts and yards of His Majesty's ships at the several Ports and to consider of the propriety of repairing, selling or breaking up of the same, and to inspect the building of His Majesty's ships in Merchants' Yards', reported Sir Oswyn Murray in his masterly *The Admiralty*.[24] Over and above those tasks which one might think were quite onerous enough as they entailed frequent visitations to all the Dockyards involved, he was required to sit as a member of one of the three sub-committees into which the Board's total of nine commissioners were divided; and to be in attendance at the launchings of ships of significance. In Seppings' case, he was also a major innovator in shipbuilding practices, an experimenter in new techniques in such matters as the preservation of timber, and an innovative ship designer.

---

[22] See Appendix II for the complete text of this Memorial.
[23] The words 'Navy Office' were engraved above the main entrance to its premises in Somerset House.
[24] Murray, *The Admiralty*, Part VI, Mariner's Mirror, Vo. 24, No. 3, 1938.

Although from the beginning of his tenure in the top office Seppings was able to influence the design of ships and bring in innovations in shipbuilding practices for a number of years into the future, many 'old' ship designs were still used, as is shown by the following story about HMS *Trincomalee*. Back in 1794 Seppings' mentor, John Henslow designed the *Leda* class of 38-gun frigates along the lines of the French *Hebe*, a prize captured in 1782. A measure of their success is that for over a quarter of a century about 40 of this class were constructed of which HMS *Trincomalee* was one. She deserves special mention here for two reasons; she is still afloat to this day and, when she was finally launched in 1817, some of Robert Seppings improvements, i.e. iron knees and their associated attachments, were incorporated into her build. In 1812 the Admiralty decided to build two of the class at the Bombay Dockyard owned by the famous Parsee shipwright, Jamsetjee Bomanjee Wadia. The plans were taken aboard HMS *Java*, Captain Henry Lambert. At that time Britain was at war with the United States in the so-called 'Naval War of 1812' (which in fact lasted from June 1812 until December 1814, although the peace only became official after being ratified by both nations in February 1815). Off St. Salvador (Brazil) on the penultimate day of December 1812, *Java* sighted the more heavily armed USS *Constitution*, and after a two hour battle the mortally wounded Lambert ordered his flag struck. The survivors were taken aboard the American vessel after which the badly damaged *Java* was set on fire. In the following year a second set reached Bombay safely and HMS *Trincomalee*, built of teak – hence her longevity – and including Seppings' iron knees, was launched in October 1817. Eighty years later she became the *Foudroyant* Training Ship, and kept that name until 1977. The restoration of the ship under her original name began in 1990. She can now be visited in Hartlepool Dock where the restoration work took place, and is the second oldest ship still afloat in the world. (HMS *Victory* is, of course, in a dry-dock.) By strange coincidence, the oldest ship still afloat happens to be the USS *Constitution*, the ship that sank the *Java*. Nicknamed 'Old Ironsides' despite being timber-built throughout, she too was once used as a training ship. She is now maintained at the Old Boston Navy Yard in Charlestown, Massachusetts, and is a commissioned vessel of the U.S. Navy.

The Navy Board with its various departments took up about one-third of the total space of the huge Somerset House complex. However, not all of it was for offices, for that part of it known as Somerset Place contained a number of apartments for senior Board members and their families, and the Surveyor resided at No.6. So once again Robert Seppings was living on the job, so to speak. However, as those apartments were provided free, were very spacious and splendidly fitted out and included servants' quarters, and were situated in the centre of London with fine river views – the Upper part of the Pool of London with all its shipping could be seen when looking eastward – one supposes that nobody concerned would have been doing any complaining.[25]

This extremely energetic man also found time to write some learned papers. In one called '*On the strength given to Ships of War by the application of Diagonal Bracing*' which he read before the Royal Society on 17 November 1814, Seppings wrote: '… if I have received any assistance in the progress of the new system, now universally adopted in the British navy, it was from the plans and drawings of the celebrated bridge at Schaffhausen, <u>and from no other source</u>.' [The present author's underlining.] It so impressed the Royal Society that later that year he was elected a Fellow, and in 1817 was awarded that body's coveted Copley Medal.

That 'celebrated bridge' over the Rhine at the Swiss town of Schaffhausen had been constructed of timber by Hans Ulrich Grubermann in 1757. (The Grubermanns were a well-known family of Swiss joiners and civil engineers.) To provide strength the structure incorporated a novel system of arches and trusses. Although the plans of it have survived, unfortunately the bridge itself has not, as it was burned down by the French during the war of 1799. (Schaffhausen, which lies on the Swiss/German border, was accidentally bombed by the American air force in 1944.)

Seppings seems later to have decided in the face of severe criticism of that single source statement, that more clarification of his sources was needed, for in a deposition made to the Admiralty dated 22 May 1818 he contradicted that statement in a not insubstantial way by listing a total of ten precedents

---

[25] It is of interest to know because it shows the importance of John Knowles' post as Chief Clerk in the Surveyor's Office, that he too had free living accommodation in Somerset House. When Knowles' friend the painter Henry Fuseli died in 1825, according to his death certificate he had been living with Fowles in Somerset House.

that had influenced his ideas on diagonal bracing. (The fact that the document was called a deposition, which is an official declaration used as a substitute for the production of a witness, seems to indicate that he was obliged to make it by order of someone in authority.) Amongst the ten precedents he now named was the work of Gabriel Snodgrass, a man mentioned in passing in Chapter 1.

Snodgrass was another man of considerable genius in the shipbuilding world, but one who though well known in his own time, has now been largely forgotten. He was born in 1720, possibly in North Petherwin, Cornwall, and later lived at Chatham in Kent. In 1735 at a premium of £10, he was apprenticed to a shipwright called Isaac Snell at Deptford.[26] Snell, a Devonian from the village of Stoke Damerel, who in 1711 had been apprenticed at Plymouth to Arthur Slade a member of a well known family of shipwrights, was a 'builder's measurer', a distinct and important specialist occupation within the shipwright trade.[27] (The measurer was the man with the duty of ensuring that the dimensions of every part of a ship's structure conformed to the specifications outlined in that most holy of holies, the Mould Loft.) Snell passed his considerable skills on to Snodgrass who completed his apprenticeship in 1742, and some years later he was 'recommended into the service of the Honourable East India Company (HEIC)' by Benjamin Slade. He then spent about ten years as superintendent of shipping at Calcutta, the company's headquarters on the sub-continent. As well as superintending the building of ships at that place, as the company also used shipbuilding and repairing facilities in other parts of India, it is more than likely that he visited those at Bombay and so was influenced by the good practices he saw there. Back home in 1757 he was promoted Surveyor to the HEIC, a post equivalent to that of the same name at the Admiralty, a position he held until his retirement in 1794.[28]

Such was Snodgrass's standing in shipbuilding circles, that in March 1771 he was called upon to give his views on the subject to a Committee of the House of Commons. He spoke of the shipbuilding timber shortage problem, and delivered a paper concerning his general ideas 'with respect to promoting

---

[26] Apprentice's Register IR 1, 14, f 1, National Archives.

[27] Apprentice's Register IR 1, 41 f 131.

[28] In 1768 another one-time Royal Dockyard apprentice called John Brent (1729-1812) was made his assistant. Brent went on to become a partner in Randall & Brent, a notable shipyard at Rotherhithe on the Thames.

the growth, and reducing the consumption of, oak timber'. He also recommended that, 'the King's ships be built in docks under a roof', to help rid the industry of the perennial problem of wood-rot. We shall see that here he anticipated Seppings' own work in those areas by well over twenty years. He also introduced iron knees into the construction of HEIC ships a long time before Seppings was allowed to do so in the navy, and improved the seaworthiness of those same vessels by doing away with the raised forecastle and poops, so introducing what were called flush deck vessels.

In 1791 he proposed to the Admiralty that they stiffened older ships 'with diagonal braces in the transverse plane, and doubling with 3 inch oak planking to increase the shear strength', wrote David K. Brown.[29] This suggestion, the one Seppings came to list in his precedents, was not taken up until 1805, as we shall see below.

Snodgrass was extremely patriotic and in a memorial to the Admiralty dated 9 March 1796, the year of his retirement from the HEIC, he decried British naval shipwrights' penchant for designing ships to the patterns of vessels captured from the French. He wrote:

> 'I am of the opinion that a great deal too much has been said in favour of French ships. I cannot myself see anything worthy of being copied from them but their magnitude; they are in other respects much inferior to British ships of war, being slighter and weaker, in general draw more water, and they likewise commonly exceed the old ships of the present navy in the absurd tumble-home of their topsides.'

Gabriel Snodgrass died in 1799 (see box below) and so was not around when the controversy over the matter of the invention of diagonal trussing developed during the first two decades of the 19th century, a controversy that has not been conclusively settled to this day. When Seppings expanded his list of precedents to include Snodgrass's name, he must have recalled that when still serving as Master Shipwright and working on putting his own system into HMS *Kent* at Chatham between May and November 1805, that his opposite number at Portsmouth Dockyard had, at long last, been ordered to use the Snodgrass system of bracing in HMS *Bellona* during its refit at that port between April and June of that very same year. Although the two systems had considerable differences (the principal one being that the Seppings system was in the longitudinal plane, the other in the transverse), there were

---

[29] Snodgrass entry in DNB.

certain similarities including the aim of both systems, which was to increase the longitudinal strength of ships. The Master Shipwrights at those two places must have known of each other's work, for at that time it was a matter of especial national importance.

From early in that year of 1805, Britain had been in the throes of a full-blown invasion scare. French troops were massing at ports on the Channel and the so-called Combined Franco-Spanish Fleet under Admiral Villeneuve who was to cover the invasion, was somewhere out at sea. Although Nelson, flying his flag in HMS *Victory*, was in hot pursuit of that fleet, Britain was in turmoil. In Parliament questions were continuously being asked about the readiness of the navy: in fact the Government and the Admiralty were under fire from all directions. Under that pressure the Royal Navy, short of ships, had perforce to drag every available one back into service, even old ones like *Bellona* a 74-gun 3rd Rate dating from 1760 which was almost falling to pieces. The Admiralty decided that the quickest way to stiffen *Bellona*'s ancient frames was to use the ideas put forward by Gabriel Snodgrass. According to Peter Goodwin, one-time curator of HMS *Victory*, in his book *The Ships of Trafalgar*, other vessels amongst the assortment of the twenty-seven that were hurried to sea at the time, also received the Snodgrass treatment; '… some were furnished with diagonal bracing recommended to the Admiralty by Gabriel Snodgrass', he wrote. He went on, 'This salient point proves that the introduction of diagonal bracing, generally referred to as the Seppings System, cannot be accredited wholly to Robert Seppings'.

Gabriel Snodgrass married a lady called Mary in about 1760. They had a house built at Blackheath, then in Kent, a favourite place for HEIC officials to build their residences. 'He built himself a handsome house with a fabulous river view at the top of Blackheath Hill, still there and now known as No. 89', wrote Beryl Platts in her *History of Greenwich* in 1973. The house of four stories including an attic, is now a Grade II listed building. The Snodgrass's had a son and two daughters. The son, called Thomas, was born in 1761. He worked at Madras for many years in HEIC's Civil Service department. He married and had a son also called Thomas who worked in India too. One of Gabriel's daughters called Sarah, married a widower called John Jeffery of Poole, in St. Alfege Church, Greenwich in October 1799. (Jeffery was Mayor of Poole in 1818 and again in 1823 and was a Member of Parliament.) Mary Snodgrass died in 1798, her husband Gabriel a year later. These are the words of the inscription on their memorial in the graveyard of St. Luke's Church, Charlton, close to Blackheath.

'In memory of Gabriel Snodgrass an old and faithful servant of the East India Company, born 5 January 1720, died 30 June 1799. Also to the memory of his consort Mary, born 17 January 1742, died 16 March 1798. Both excellent in all conditions of human life, may their souls rest in Heavenly peace. This monument is erected by their dutiful and affectionate son, Thomas.'

Across the way there is another memorial. The words on that one read, 'In the vault beneath are deposited the remains of their son, Thomas Snodgrass Esq. of Chesterfield Road, Mayfair, late of the HEIC's Civil Service at Madras who departed this life 28 August 1834 in the 73rd year of his age.' It is perhaps worth recording that according to Beryl Platts (and others), Charles Dickens when he came to write his *Pickwick Papers* in 1836, took Gabriel's surname for his character Mr. Augustus Snodgrass, the one who was always about to write a poem but never got around to writing a single stanza.

As previously noted, in regard to Snodgrass, Robert Seppings had corrected himself over the precedents that had influenced his diagonal trussing system. However, he made no mention in his new list, a list that included a number of notable foreign shipbuilders including the Swedish Fredrik Chapman, of a certain William May of Amsterdam and it seems he should have.[30]

William May (1725-1807) was a third generation shipbuilding émigré from Britain. Because of the family's foreign origins none of them were ever popular on the continent though that had not prevented May from being appointed Dockyard Superintendent to the Amsterdam Admiralty in 1780, a post he was to hold for fifteen years. Sometime before 1784 he presented his ideas on a system of longitudinal diagonal trussing to the frames of ships,

---

[30] Fredrik Henrik af Chapman (1721-1808) – the af indicates he had been ennobled by the Swedish king – was probably the most mathematical minded of all shipwrights of his time, having studied mathematics for two years in Stockholm, followed by a year in London. A treatise he had written on shipbuilding was translated into English in 1820 by the Rev. James Inman who was himself a mathematician of note and of whom more will be said in this book.

to the Amsterdam Admiralty. None of the original documents have survived, but they were associated with a model of a ship-of-the line which has, and which is now on display at the Ryksmuseum in Amsterdam. Part of the model is 'open' – that is the hull is not planked over – so one can see a complete depiction of May's bracing system, a system that was actually used in the construction of the 64-gun ship *Leiden* at Amsterdam in 1784/1785. Could that ship have influenced Seppings ideas? We shall see that the answer to that question must be in the affirmative.

In 1799 an Anglo-Russian naval force invaded what was then called the Batavian Republic in the Netherlands. During that expedition Vice Admiral Andrew Mitchell's squadron captured twenty-five Batavian vessels, including sixteen ships-of-the-line. One of the latter was the *Leiden*, which was taken into the Royal Navy as HMS *Leyden*. According to Dutch historian Dr. Alan Lemmers in his article *Shipworm, Hogbacks and Duck's Arses: The Influence of William May on Sir Robert Seppings* (a source which has been of considerable help to the present author), *Leyden* was 'brought into Chatham for refit in ordinary' in May 1805.

That happened to be the same month in which Robert Seppings began his work aboard HMS *Kent* in that very same dockyard. Dr. Lemmers mentioned the drawings held at the National Maritime Museum at Greenwich, of Seppings' rebuild of the *Kent*. They show that oblique riders were included, that sloped aft in the fore part of the ship, and forward in the after end, just as they did in the former Dutch vessel (and in May's model referred to earlier). 'Seppings' rebuild of HMS *Kent* looks very much like May's system in the *Leiden*', wrote Lemmers, before adding, 'the simultaneous refit of the *Leiden* is too much of a coincidence to ignore'. Bearing in mind that every operation in a Royal Dockyard (except by age-old tradition, the ropemaking and sailmaking departments) came under the supervision of the Master Shipwright, there is no possibility that Seppings could have been unaware of the *Leiden*'s unique construction. Dr. Lemmers was being rather generous when he recorded that Seppings possibly omitted to mention the *Leiden* as a precedent, 'because he did not know who had devised the construction'.

We must stay on William May for a while longer as we discuss more fully the change from the square-built ship stern with all its weaknesses including its restriction on field of fire, to the circular-shaped, pinched-in one known as a duck's arse, which suffered from less of those weaknesses. These sterns were not new in small to medium sized vessels in a number of shipbuilding countries. In Holland, May's adopted country, for example, the *hoeker* or *houckboot* (hooker in English) mostly used in the North Atlantic cod fisheries, had been constructed with pinched-in sterns since about 1600. Around 1780 May submitted plans accompanied by a model (another one now in the Rijksmuseum), for a hooker-shaped frigate, but the plans were rejected. Then, in about 1790, May befriended a young Danish naval architect called Frantz Hohlenberg, and there is good evidence to show that May passed the plans for his ship with a more circular stern over to the Dane. According to Dr. Lemmers, Hohlenberg later wrote of having been inspired by a Dutchman in his design of a pinched-in stern, and says that Dutchman could only have been May. There is more evidence in the portraits of May and Hohlenberg reproduced in this book, which were described by Lemmers as 'a set of counterparts'.[31] The one of May depicts him holding a scroll of documents bearing the legend in English, 'Naval Architecture. For my Learned Friend H. Hohlenberg'. The Hohlenberg portrait depicts him holding a drawing on which is written 'W. May Captain ter Zee invenit'.

A decade later, at Copenhagen between 1800 and 1803, the 90-gun *Christian VII* was constructed to Hohlenberg's design, which included May's type of stern. This ship was captured by the British in 1807, and subsequently commissioned into the Royal Navy in 1808 under the same name. The ship still had a square transom, but one much narrower than usual, and because the British found it both 'curious and interesting', descriptions of it must soon have passed around the Royal Dockyards. As Hohlenberg's design was influenced by William May, and as the 80-gun HMS *Cambridge* built at Deptford between 1813 and 1815 during the first years of Robert Seppings' reign as Surveyor, was a 'faithful copy' of the *Christian VII*, there is a link albeit an indirect one, with Seppings' final version of his own circular stern, a link that was the basis of that charge of 'pilfering' mentioned by Sir John Barrow, Secretary of the Admiralty which was quoted in the Foreword to this book.

It will be useful at this point to repeat Barrow's words, but in full this time. They come from his book *A Family Tour Through South Holland*, a tour he made in 1828 during which he made a semi-official visit to the naval dockyard in Rotterdam. He wrote of that visit:

---

[31] The pair of paintings are unsigned. Adriaan de Lelie (1755-1820) has been mentioned as the possible artist.

'Under a second roof was a fifty-gun frigate building, and under a third, one of the same class repairing. The new frigate had a round stern, similar to which Sir Robert Seppings was accused of having pilfered from the Dutch, but which, though perhaps superior for all naval purposes, he had reconverted almost to square ones, reserving however, the principle of upright timbers, which by giving strength constitutes its greatest merit.'

He went on to mention a number of other technical differences between the Dutch and Seppings' versions of the more-rounded stern, which in his view clearly absolved Seppings from the charge of pilfering. He also observed other aspects of the work being carried out in that Dutch yard, and made this rather telling remark:

'In short it appeared to us that the whole of Seppings' inventions had been adopted in the dockyard of Rotterdam.'

He went on to visit the yards in Amsterdam, and then wrote:

'On observing to our conductor that it appeared they had adopted all our late improvements here and at Rotterdam – round sterns, diagonal braces etc., he said they could not follow a better example. (That officer had worked in Deptford dockyard for several years.)'

(The first edition of this particular book by the prolific Sir John Barrow was published anonymously in 1831, when Seppings was out of favour with the Admiralty and nearing the end of his tenure in office.)

We have seen that it is often very difficult to distinguish between a so-called 'new' invention and an improvement on, or an adaptation of, another's work. With Seppings, because in the case of his diagonal stiffening of ships and also in the case of his circular stern, there were substantial and significant differences in his final versions from those of any of his rivals in the field, it seems he always considered his work different enough to be considered new.

Let us hear what John Knowles had to say about all this in a letter written in July 1822 to the editor of the *Monthly Magazine & British Register*. It was in reply to a letter by someone calling himself 'Fact', published in the May 1822 edition of the magazine. Knowles' letter appeared under the heading, '*Mr. Knowles in Defence of Sir Robert Seppings*'. He wrote that his own Appendix on Seppings' work, (appended to Steel's book as mentioned earlier), had been used as a text by 'Fact', 'for the purposes of abusing the inventor, and of conveying to your readers the notion that all the improvements which he had introduced are due to the ingenuity of others'.[32] He then set about showing that most of what 'Fact' had written was not true, and that although there had been other attempts to solve the problems, so that,

> 'Most of the principles have been long known and practised, and thus have become public property; but if the limits of a letter would allow, I could show very material modifications and alterations in each, as introduced by Sir Robert Seppings, so as to give them the title of inventions.
> 'In the hands of the persons who preceded him, these alterations from the common system failed; under his management and by his improvements they have succeeded admirably.
> 'And it is always to be recollected, that it is the whole machine which is to be regarded, not its parts; and although we cannot create a new mechanical power, yet every credit is due to him who unveils a useful machine by a new combination of known principles.'

It can be said that before Seppings, all previous attempts to solve the problem of strengthening the hulls of ships had not been complete systems and so had not solved the overall problem. Moreover, Seppings' systems were the ones that came to be used in the Royal Navy, the largest and most potent instrument of sea power the world had ever known, systems that were soon copied by shipbuilders, naval and mercantile, throughout the maritime world. Looking at all the available evidence through modern eyes and with the benefit of hindsight, we can sum up by saying that had he taken a little more care in listing the factors and people that had influenced his work – it is surely never shameful to have sources of inspiration – he would have suffered less accusations of plagiarism and therefore less personal stress and strain, just as the ships for which he was responsible for building and repairing, suffered less stress and strain. Perhaps 'Old Gabriel' as Snodgrass was dubbed in the *United Services Magazine* in 1836, and the brilliant but now virtually forgotten émigré William May, will sleep more easily in their

---

[32] That letter by 'Fact' included a remark about Seppings' salary as Surveyoy in 1822. It was £1,000 per annum.

graves, if we now allow them some of the credit.[33] (May died in 1807 at Cleves in Germany, the place where Anne, the fourth wife of Henry VIII, was born in the 16th century.)

Whilst on the subject of the controversies that developed over some of the inventions and improvements made by Robert Seppings, it is worthwhile pointing out that he was never backward in encouraging inventions by others in the naval dockyards, and in recommending appropriate awards when they were deserved. He secured, for example, £250 for a Master Painter called Anderson at Portsmouth for a new method of mixing paint used for timber preservation.

---

[33] Gabriel Snodgrass, according to the anonymous person who wrote his obituary in the *European Magazine* Vol. 36 of 1799, was a very modest man, and one of those whose talents never received 'the best reward'. That writer went on, 'What praise is due to him by whose exertion and application thousands have navigated in remote seas with safety and security.'

5
Some Protégés and Followers: His Relationship with the School of Naval Architecture

Robert Seppings' post of Surveyor, together with his fellowship of the Royal Society from 1814, presented him with many opportunities to make contacts amongst the great and good of the land. By happenstance the headquarters of the Royal Society at that time was also in Somerset House, and for many years the President of the Society was the celebrated Sir Joseph Banks who had in fact, channelled the publication in *Philosophical Transactions* of the paper Seppings had read before the Society which led to his Fellowship. According to H.B. Carter, Banks' major biographer, 'Seppings was a naval designer in whom Banks had great confidence'.[34] Not only was Banks a personal friend of King George, he had his finger in so many governmental pies that if there was anyone in the realm worth having the good opinion of, it was he. All the Society's main meetings took place at Somerset House, and its annual dinners were held just around the corner at the *Crown and Anchor* in the Strand; there was also a Royal Society Dinner Club, whose members, perhaps including Seppings either as a member or a guest, met monthly at the *Mitre* tavern in Fleet Street. We shall see that for a while he worked closely on a project with another FRS, the scientist Sir Humphry Davy.

At the beginning of 1816 when Rear Admiral Sir Thomas Byam Martin was appointed Comptroller of the Navy Board, even more doors opened for Robert Seppings (both figuratively and literally because Byam Martin also lived and worked in Somerset House). Seppings with his powerful personality, great ability and hard-work ethic (and rather intimidating gaze if his portraits are anything to go by), found a kindred spirit in Byam Martin, and for the best part of the next two decades the two men who became fast friends, came to dominate the Board, a board that arguably reached its highest ever degree of efficiency under them, and furthermore one which worked in harmony with the incumbent First Lord of the Admiralty (then Lord Melville) which had not always been the case.

---

[34] Carter, Sir Joseph Banks p. 499.

An indication of what can be called the scientific nature of much of his work came in February 1817 with his attempts to measure deflections in a ship's structure. In a trial onboard HMS *Justitia* (built in Denmark in 1777 and captured in 1807), which was about to be broken up at Portsmouth, he had 'temporary bracing placed in the opposite, compressive, direction to that usually adopted, [it] still produced a deflection, but confirmed him in his view was best suited as its members were in tension', wrote the author of an article on Seppings in 2002. That author went on, 'These observations although in the field of Naval Architecture, were among the earliest on such large structures, and reflect his practical approach to engineering design. In modern parlance he developed a reinforced membrane capable of resisting shear force, although much of the theoretical discussion was on beam behaviour.'[35]

Small wonder that the House of Common's Financial Select Committee in 1819, had remarked,

'Your committee deem it their particular duty to notice Mr. Seppings, one of the surveyors of the navy, to whose abilities and exertions this country is mainly indebted for many of its most valuable improvements in Naval Architecture.'

Along the way, this once unlikely lad from Norfolk received other plaudits and honours in the form of valuable gifts from such leaders as Tsar Alexander of Russia, King William I of Holland, and King Frederick VI of Denmark. (Some of these gifts are still in the hands of family descendants.) But the culminating honour came on 17 August 1819 when during a right royal naval occasion, he was knighted by the King's third son, Prince William Henry, Duke of Clarence, the Prince Regent who later became the 'Sailor King', William IV. The ceremony took place aboard HM yacht *Royal George*, the craft being 'under sail, the royal standard flying'. It seems that Seppings had written the Memorial of his services dated 1 March 1819 (which has already been quoted from and which appears in its entirety in Appendix II), at the Prince Regent's request as a prerequisite for that honour.

In 1810, in an endeavour to raise the general quality of shipbuilding in Britain, the Admiralty School of Naval Architecture was founded at Portsmouth. Between 1815-1817 a special building was built for it in the southwest corner of the dockyard across the way from the Naval Academy for Naval Officers (built 1733). The school signed up 25 students annually, and

---

[35] Skempton, ed.

its first Principal was the Rev. James Inman, Professor of Nautical Mathematics at the Naval Academy. He brought with him a syllabus that tended more towards the scientific and mathematical than the practical side of the profession, and that was something to which most shipwrights took exception.[36] But there was something else that most of the old-timers did not like about the school. Its students were virtually apprenticed to the Admiralty itself and so not to individual shipwrights, and that ate into and undermined the hoary old money-making system of personal apprentices. Even though by that Order in Council of May 1801 mentioned earlier, the practice of the Master pocketing his apprentice's wages in Royal shipyards had been done away with, shipwrights were still able to influence entry into the profession and obtain premiums for taking apprentices on, but not of course, for those at the new school. Robert Seppings, who was still Master Shipwright at Chatham at the time and who had his own apprentices, was one of the few senior members of his profession to support the school's establishment, seeing in it the best way to raise overall standards. In fact it can been said he was influential in its founding, for he had given evidence in support of it before the Commission of Naval Revision in 1810. It is recorded that his son, John Milligen Seppings, sat for the school's entry examination and did not pass, but his son's failure seems not to have caused him to alter his positive stance about the school.

His support for it is indicated in the career of one of its students, William McPherson Rice (1796-1853). Rice entered the school in 1813 and graduated as a shipwright in 1819. He then spent three years at various Royal Dockyards, before becoming draughtsman to Seppings in 1822. In that same year under an order signed by Comptroller Sir Byam Martin, and no doubt on the recommendation of Seppings, he was sent to conduct a survey of the remains of an old vessel discovered under the former bed of the River Rother in Kent. Rice's report was a brilliant and learned piece of archaeological research into this vessel (it was a 14th century English trading craft) that eventually appeared in the journal *Archaeologia* and for which he was made a Fellow of the Society of Arts.[37] In 1824 he was sent out on a special mission, no doubt again with Seppings' blessing, to Rio de Janeiro to 'put a new mast together' for HMS *Spartiate*, which was then Rear Admiral Sir George Eyre's flagship on station there. After he returned he was promoted Foreman at

---

[36] James Inman (1776-1859). A book compiled under his guidance, known as Inman's *Nautical Tables*, was still being used by some navigators well into the 20th century.

[37] *Archaeologia*, Vol.22. The identification of this craft as English came well after Rice's time.

Chatham Dockyard, on a salary of £250 per annum, and in the following year married a lady called Fanny Turner. They had six children. In 1837 he was sent in the paddle-steamer HMS *Columbia* to Lough Swilly on the north coast of Ireland where HMS *Terror*, badly damaged from having been trapped in Arctic ice for the best part of a year, had been run ashore. He advised Captain George Back on the best way to repair and refloat the ship after which she was towed back to Chatham. He was promoted Assistant Master Shipwright in 1844, and was stationed at Portsmouth Dockyard at the time of the 1851 Census, in which he described himself as Naval Assistant in that yard. He was appointed Master Shipwright, Pembroke Dock in 1852. He died at Halton, near Hastings in 1868 and was buried in St. Clement's Church in that place.

It was mentioned when talking about the charges of plagiarism laid at Seppings' door, how sometimes it is difficult to separate invention from improvements and adaptions. This was well illustrated when Seppings ensured that Captain Wells of the *Glory* was given credit for the idea of adapting his dry-dock wedge system for use as a fid in lifting out a ship's top-gallant mast. William McPherson Rice, provides us, without taking credit for an 'invention', of an improvement on an adaption! Writing in the *United Service Journal* in 1831, Rice described "a method long-practised in the merchant navy for fidding top-gallant masts, by introducing two wedges one upon the other, in the square fid-hole". Rice had examined the use made of this system in ships of the Hon. East India Company and by Captain Sir Benjamin Hallowell in HMS *Prince Regent* in about 1825, and had then gone on to design what he himself described as an 'improvement' which he submitted to the Navy Board in December 1829, which was approved by that body (of which Seppings was a member), and subsequently tried out in both HMS *Ganges* and HMS *Gannet* (and in the East Indiaman *George Canning*), after which it became a standard fitting in most ships. It should be noted that although Rice described his system only as an 'improvement', the editor of the *USJ* in an introduction, called it an 'invention'.[38]

This mention of Rice's improvement is of particular importance because on 6th May 1826, Sir Robert had taken out a Royal patent on 'a system

---

[38] Rice, *A Key-fid for Striking Topmasts and Top-Gallant masts*: etc, etc.

of fids or apparatus for striking Top Masts and Top Gallant masts in ships'.[39]

It seems rather unfortunate that the School of Naval Architecture lasted only for a little over two decades. It was closed in 1832 because 'too much science and too little practical knowledge' had crept into the industry, wrote Edward Fraser in his *British Watercraft* series in the *Mariner's Mirror*. We shall see later that the money that had been expended on that establishment was also a contentious issue.

We know something about the career of one of the apprentices Robert took on during the second decade of the 1800s. There were probably more, for there is little doubt there would have been a queue of aspiring acolytes for a man who, year by year, was growing more famous in his profession. That apprentice was Thomas Ditchburn, born in 1801. In an announcement of Ditchburn's death in the *Gravesend & Dartford Reporter* for 21 May 1870 we read, 'he was a favourite of Sir Robert Seppings, being much employed in making models and trying experiments'. Given the usual starting age, his apprenticeship probably began in 1815 and ended in 1822. Within a few years of 'passing out' he left Admiralty service to become manager of the commercial shipbuilding firm of Fletcher & Fearnall at Hogs Yard, Limehouse on the River Thames. In 1837 he went into partnership with a certain C.J. Mare, and as Ditchburn & Mare, took over Dudman's Yard at Deptford. After that yard was gutted by fire, the firm moved to larger premises at Orchard Yard, Blackwall, where it concentrated on building steamships, and between 1836-46 constructed over fifty including eight for the Admiralty, one of which was a Royal Yacht called *Fairy*, a craft often used to ferry important guests across the Solent to Queen Victoria's hideaway, Osborne House on the Isle of Wight. In 1846 Ditchburn retired at the age of only 45, but the firm went on under the management of C.J. Mare to build much larger ships with a great deal of success until it fell into decline in 1855 after underestimating on an Admiralty contract for six gunboats. Under an expanded management team the firm got back on its feet to such an extent that its tender in 1859 to build HMS *Warrior*, the British navy's first iron-clad, was accepted. Soon after that the firm became known as the Thames Ironworks and Shipbuilding Co. Ltd., and went on to become one of the most successful private shipyards ever to grace the banks of the River Thames.

[39] Information taken from Sir Robert's illuminated copy of the Royal patent concerned, and used here by permission of Mrs. Christine Colthurst.

It built dreadnoughts and other iron warships, not only for Britain, but also for Russia, Turkey, Greece, Portugal, Japan, Prussia and Spain. The firm carried on until 1912 when all such work finished on the Thames.

We come now to John Milligen Seppings', Robert's eldest son born at Plymouth in 1796. No record has been found of any formal apprenticeship for him, but it appears likely that his training was taken in hand by his father in about 1810 when he was fourteen, perhaps soon after that failed effort to get him into Inman's school. After his promotion to Surveyor, Robert would have been able to use considerable influence in the furtherance of his son's career and for reasons that will become clear, it is also safe to assume that John soon began specializing in draughtsmanship, perhaps working alongside his father in Somerset House. If all that was so, then young Seppings would have passed out as a shipwright in 1817 at the age of twenty-one. After that he probably increased his experience by spending more time in shipyards and in his father's office.

He must have shown exceptional promise because in 1820 the members of the council of the Honourable East India Company offered him the post of Superintendent of Shipping at Bengal. No doubt Robert Seppings used his contacts and friendships with council members to get them to consider his son for the post, but the HEIC, who tended to employ only the best, would not have made the offer had they not been impressed by his abilities. So, later that year, John Milligen Seppings sailed out to Calcutta to make his fortune – the Company always paid well and there were also substantial perquisites to be made, ones officially sanctioned to compensate for the high death rate amongst its employees stationed on the Indian sub-continent. (It should be noted Seppings' post was the one once held by Gabriel Snodgrass.)

The next firm information we have about John appeared in the *Asiatic Journal and Monthly Register*, quoting the *Calcutta Government Gazette* for 12 October 1821.

> The launch of the teak-built, 835 ton *William Money*, Captain Jackson, took place at Kiddapore; built by James and Robert Kyd under the superintendence of Mr. Seppings.

Then on 16 May 1823 he married, and the following announcement appeared in the *Calcutta Government Gazette*.

> At St. John's Cathedral, Calcutta, by the Rev. J. Parson, John Milligen Seppings, Esq. Surveyor in the Marine Department, eldest son of Sir

Robert Seppings, one of the Commissioners of His Majesty's Navy, to
Marianne Matthews, youngest daughter of the late Francis Robert
Matthews of Brompton, Middlesex.
(The couple had issue in India of which full details will be found in the
Seppings' family details in Appendix 1).

On 16 February 1827 the following report was published in Calcutta.
New steamer *Ganges* launched yesterday from Kyd dockyard at
Kiddapore is one of two vessels that were ordered by the Supreme
Government to be constructed for the Honourable Company. Same as
Irawaddy launched on New Year's Day. Both vessels built under the
immediate directions of Mr. Seppings the Hon. Company's surveyor.
The drawings of the vessels were originally prepared by Sir Robert
Seppings the Surveyor of His Majesty's Navy. Found necessary to alter
them for the climate and the present design is by Mr. Seppings, the
eldest son of Sir Robert. Mr. Seppings invited contracts from the
different builders on the River Hooghly. Launched in the presence of
His Excellency Lord Combermere. [Field Marshal Viscount Combermere
of Bhurtpore, Commander-in-Chief, India.]

This indicates that with the permission of the Admiralty, Sir Robert Seppings
had designed at least two vessels for the HEIC. We shall see (in Chapter 7)
that although he did not receive a fee for this work, he was recompensed in
another way. (The use of Sir Robert's shipbuilding principles had begun at
Calcutta eight years earlier when Kyd & Co. built the 1,732 ton *Warren
Hastings* there. That ship was built of teak to the order of a shareholding
consortium of 63 local businessmen, '24 British, 21 Indian, 12 Armenian
and 6 Portuguese'.[40])

It is known from one of Sir Robert's letters, that in 1833 John Milligen
Seppings, his wife Marianne and their children, were in England on leave.
(HEIC employees based in India were permitted local leaves of absence once
a year, during which they made for the coolness of one or other of the famous
Indian hill stations, and periodical long leaves, possibly every five years, in
England for which they travelled home in HEIC ships but at their own
expense. As a guide to the substantial travel costs involved, in 1810 the fares

---

[40] *East India Register* for 1819. When this ship reached England in 1819 she was purchased
by the Admiralty and commissioned into the navy as the 74-gun HMS *Hastings*. The
navy valued the ship at a lower figure than her building cost, so if those 63 shareholders
had expected to make a profit on the sale, they were disappointed.

for officers in the Company's own army were between £95 for a cadet and £250 for a general, significant sums in those days, and furthermore those figures were for a one-way passage only.[41]) It is more than possible that when John returned to India after that leave, he travelled alone, leaving his wife to look after the three children whilst they were educated in England; for that was usual procedure for expatriates.

During his period of nearly twenty-five years service with the HEIC, John Milligen Seppings designed and superintended the building of a number of other ships at Calcutta including the steamer *Hooghly* in 1825, three opium clippers called the *Sylph*, *Rob Roy*, and the largest one, the *Cowasgee* of 431 tons in the 1830s, and in that same decade, a pilot brig and a light-vessel. These vessels were listed in a work by John Phipps of the Master Attendant's Office, Calcutta in 1840, which included a note to the effect that all these vessels were 'built on Sir Robert Seppings' new principles'.[42]

That tome of John Phipps' also included a long, very detailed and learned treatise entitled *Indian Timbers and Shipbuilding* written by John M. Seppings in 1837. It compared the merits of the various forms of teak available to Indian shipbuilders, such as the local Sawl (or Sal) and Sinoo, and also two varieties that came from farther afield, Pegu [Burma] teak and Java teak. It discussed the problem of the havoc played on various timbers (but not teak because insects do not like the natural oil in it) by white ants. He wrote that he had tried steaming them out, and that even using the treatment for two days, did not 'extirpate them'. In that work Seppings showed that he had probably become the leading European expert on the subject of Eastern woods used in shipbuilding. If the reader will excuse a pun, it can truly be said that he was a chip off the old block, because as we shall see in the next chapter, his father was intimately involved in all aspects of what was known in Britain as the 'Timber Problem'.

In April 1838 the *East India Register* reported that, 'Mr. J.M. Seppings surveyor of shipping in Bengal, to England for two years for health. Mr. Joseph Simpson to execute duties of Mr. Seppings as surveyor during Mr. Seppings' absence'. In 1841 the *Register* announced that Seppings had returned from England on 18 February 1841. Perhaps his health soon began to deteriorate again for within two years he was on his way home again, this time never to return. He died at Torquay, Devon in 1863.

---

[41] Sutton, *Lords of the East.*
[42] Phipps, *A Collection of Papers relative to Shipbuilding in India.*

Robert Seppings had become something of a celebrity and in consequence enjoyed many of the trappings that went with that status. The marriage of his eldest daughter Martha on 17 August 1817 at the age of 21 was quite an affair, with the bride leaving Somerset Place in some style to be married in St. George's, Hanover Square, to Captain (later Major) James Hull Harrison of the Royal Marines. They had ten children. (Faith Harrison who married J.J. Packard, compiler of the Packard Papers, was descended from their eldest son Robert Harrison who became a colonel of Marines. For more information see Appendix 1.)

In June of the following year a less happy event took place at the family residence, for the *London Globe* edition for 15 April 1819, reported the following:

At the Old Bailey

Mary Ann Butler was indicted and found guilty of stealing a gallon of wine in the house of Sir Robert Seppings on 5 June last. Timothy Francis Scammel was in the service of Sir Robert in June last, and had been for two months; the family were absent from town and only the witness and the prisoner were in the house. Prisoner had departed the witness to get his tea ready in the kitchen, and he having done so, went up stairs to tell her when he saw her upon a chair trying to open the wardrobe door in which Lady Seppings kept the keys of the store cupboard, the wine-cellar, etc., with a piece of wire. Witness said, 'Mary I hope you are not opening the door to get the keys. Mary replied, she was and it was no sin to take things from Lady Seppings who had not been a very good mistress to them'. Witness afterwards saw her come down stairs with the keys in her hand; she went to the cellar and took out four bottles of wine, one of which she opened and poured out a tea-cup full which she wanted witness to drink, but he would not. The witness underwent a severe examination by Mr. Affry who endeavoured to show that his evidence was altogether a fabrication arising out of the hatred which he bore the prisoner on account of her differing from him in religious principles, she being a Protestant and he being a Catholic. The Learned Counsel however, failed to shake his testimony, and the Jury found her guilty. The prisoner was about 23 years of age, of respectable appearance, and appeared much affected by her situation. She had solemnly affirmed her innocence.

The newspaper did not report the sentence imposed, but given the times and the value of the stolen property, it may have been transportation. In view of what the prisoner had allegedly said about Lady Seppings, it is unlikely Sir Robert would have made any plea for leniency.

A quite different description of Lady Seppings has come down to us from one of her great-nieces called Frieda Gill, who described her as 'saintly and handsome, but of delicate health'. That same niece also gives us a rare contemporary family description of Sir Robert's character. 'His reserved and testy temper', she wrote, 'made him formidable to most of his relations, in spite of which my father and Sir Robert got on together admirably.'[43] We shall have a great deal more to say about Sir Robert's attitude towards some of his other relations.

At the end of April 1821 Sir Robert was one of a party led by the Marquess of Lothian who enjoyed the first day of the Cheltenham Races.[44] It was during the Christmas period of that same year, that his mother Lydia died at Fakenham aged 87. Because of the affection between them, we can be pretty certain he was in attendance when she was buried in Fakenham Churchyard on 31 December.

London's *Morning Advertiser* for 17 September 1824 informs us that he was one of the directors of the Royal National Bath Company of 1, Lancaster Place, Waterloo Bridge, founded to build extensive baths of the 'Fresh, Salt, Medicated, Vapour and Pleasure' varieties, throughout the metropolis. It had an initial capital of £250,000 made up of £50 shares, and was inviting further applications.

---

[43] Frieda Gill, *Memoirs*, mentioned in the Packard Papers. Frieda must have based her descriptions on information passed down from her father, for she was born in 1848 some years after the deaths of both Sir Robert and Lady Seppings.

[44] See *Cheltenham Chronicle*, 26 April 1821.

6
Sir Robert and the Timber Problem

Throughout his career Robert Seppings was in one way or another closely concerned with the navy's timber problem, a multi-faceted affair that included the procurement, the use and preservation of it. Upon his elevation to the post of Surveyor, the problem became one of his principle concerns.

Before we embark upon a summary of that part of his responsibilities, it may serve the reader if we first mention the end result of all the improvements he made in the structural strength of wooden ships. Those improvements, developed over several decades in a series of piece-meal measures, were at first implemented in the same piece-meal kind of way before the end result came to be incorporated into the building of every new naval ship and in the reconstruction of many of the old ones. Only then could his work be looked upon as a coherent whole. His stiffening of frames with diagonal trussing when associated with his rounded bow and more circular stern, created a significantly more rigid structure, one in which structural stresses and strains were more efficiently distributed than ever before. His changes brought other benefits too. In his article *The Reconstruction of the Royal Navy 1815-1830*,[45] Professor Andrew Lambert pointed out that, 'By keeping the ship in shape his work reduced the opportunity for movement at the joint faces, which with the removal of unseasoned timber, the prime source of decay, and the exclusion of fresh water [in the form of rain] from the hull during construction and service, brought a rapid end to the scourge of dry rot'.

The improvement in rigidity and strength also meant that the length of wooden ships could be increased. That in turn eventually led to the number of gun decks being reduced as the required number of guns could now be accommodated on just one deck or two. (As a matter of interest, the longest wooden ship ever built for the navy was HMS *Mersey*, launched at Chatham in 1858, nearly two decades after the death of Sir Robert Seppings which means he had nothing at all to do with it. At 336 feet in length she was almost twice as long as HMS *Victory*. Built with a heavy auxiliary steam engine, the weight of which along with that of the bunkering coal required, when

---

[45] Lambert, Mariner's Mirror 1996.

combined with the vessel's extreme length, placed enormous strains on the wooden hull structure, and resulted in her seams opening up. The Admiralty very soon concluded that with the *Mersey* it had exceeded the practical limits in the size of timber-built ships even though her internal construction had included many iron fittings. That led, in 1859, to the ordering of the first iron-clad, HMS *Warrior*.)

The major timber used in British shipyards throughout the age of the wooden ship was British oak. The phrases, 'wooden walls' and 'hearts of oak' are descriptive of how we British still think (and sing) about our navy during the period when, under its protective umbrella, the Empire was being created in the 18th and 19th centuries. However, throughout that period, the country was, in the words of Professor Robert G. Albion, 'dependent upon a precarious hand-to-mouth supply of native oak'.[46] And when one is reminded that 2,000 oak trees might be required to build a single ship of the 3rd Rate, the scale of the problem can better be appreciated.[47]

By the turn of the century the problem had become critical: tree fellers were now, both literally and figuratively, cutting in to what was rather euphemistically known as the nation's strategic reserve of woodlands. So-called 'compass timber', the naturally grown curved pieces needed for frames, and the crooked pieces usually found in hedgerow oaks and used for the knees that secured frames to crossbeams, were in particularly short supply. The latter shortage had been evidenced in a letter Robert Seppings wrote to the Navy Board as early as 1802 whilst he was still at Plymouth, in which he sought permission to substitute iron knees because 'no oak hanging knees were available for the repair of the gun and upper decks of the *Culloden* and *Tonnant*'. It is not clear from the records whether this permission was granted, but it is known that over the matter of iron knees the Navy Board as late as April 1804, advised its members to act with caution, stating that, 'However eligible plans which have from time to time been suggested, the result has not always answered the expectations formed from them'. (The use of iron for this purpose was by no means new. Gabriel Snodgrass, for example, had used iron knees in HEIC ships since the 1780s, and the French navy first experimented with them – they called them *courbes de fer* – sixty years before that.)

---

[46] Albion, *Timber Problem of the Royal Navy 1652-1862*, Mariner's Mirror 1952.
[47] It was reported that in excess of 5,000 trees were felled to build HMS *Victory*. A veritable forest.

Timber stocks at all dockyards had fallen to perilously low levels even before Admiral Lord St. Vincent came along in 1801 with his inopportune reforms in the dockyards that included 'taking on and sorting out' the powerful timber contractors, the profit-making middlemen in the navy's supply chain. These middlemen certainly needed sorting out but, as usual, that sour old admiral approached the task in a way that alienated every one concerned, in this case to such an extent that during most of his thankfully short time as First Lord, all timber supplies to naval yards were suspended by the contractors. (St. Vincent left the Admiralty post in May 1804. In November 1805 he was made C-in-C, Channel Fleet, and so was back on the element upon which he had always served his country best. He died in March 1823.)

When Seppings, the newly posted Master Shipwright, arrived at Chatham in 1804, he took charge of the construction of the 98-gun 2nd Rate HMS *Impregnable*, the keel of which had been laid early the year before. He spent much time trying to find timbers for her, but with little success. Four years later when compass timbers for completing that ship's frames had still not been found, Seppings proposed that shorter pieces scarphed together in a new way designed by him, be used instead. They had first been tried out in HMS *Warspite* in 1806 and were adopted throughout the navy in 1808, according to the Memorial about his services he wrote in 1819.[48] Even so, *Impregnable* was still not completed until 1810 and so had been almost eight years in the building, a long time even for a ship of that size, and caused almost entirely by the shortage of timber. Later, in the rebuild of the *Ramilles* at Chatham between 1810-1812, Seppings had to substitute pitch pine and what he called 'old timber' (probably recycled), for oak in certain places.

A good example of the lengths to which the Royal Navy was prepared to go in the hunt for useful timbers, came in 1809 during the so-called 'Great Expedition' against two of the shipbuilding-ports engaged in Napoleon's attempt to usurp Britain's position as the world's No. 1 sea-power. A combined navy/army force was sent into the River Scheldt in August to attack and destroy the dockyards at Flushing and Antwerp. Due to mismanagement and the fact that the army element was led by an incompetent called John Pitt, Earl of Chatham, it almost became a 'Great Disaster'. Although Flushing was taken, the attacking force got nowhere near Antwerp before being ordered to withdraw. Two small ships were destroyed in the shipbuilding yards at Flushing, whilst the timbers of a third, the 74-gun *Le Royal-Hollandaise*

---

[48] See R. Seppings Memorial dated 1 March 1819, reproduced in Appendix II.

1 Robert Seppings as a young boy.

2 Mrs. Lydia Seppings, Sir Robert's mother. Pencil sketch by a shipwright at Chatham, circa 1810.

3 Sir Robert Seppings' birthplace in Holt Road, Fakenham. Now called Anchor House it has been extensively altered over the years.

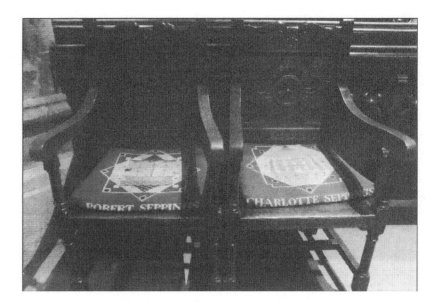

4 (above) Memorial 'bride and groom' chairs dedicated to Sir Robert and Lady Seppings in St Mary Magdelene Church, Taunton.

5 (below) Some of the gifts presented to Sir Robert Seppings by Foreign Heads of State.

4 (opposite) Memorial 'bride and groom' chairs dedicated to Sir Robert and Lady Seppings in St Mary Magdelene Church, Taunton.

5 (opposite below) Some of the gifts presented to Sir Robert Seppings by Foreign Heads of State.

6 Coat of Arms of Sir Robert Seppings.

7 Embroidered depiction of Vivary, Sir Robert's home in Taunton.

8 (opposite) Diagram showing
the main differences between
Seppings and Snodgrass methods
of strengthening ship structures.

9 (below) The 'Swan-Necked'
Miss Louisa Seppings.

10 (below right) Portrait of Gabriel
Snodgrass, Surveyor to the East India
Company.

11 (opposite below left) Portrait of
F.C. Hohlenberg, Danish Naval
Architect (1765-1804).

12 (opposite below right) Portrait of
Captain William May, Dockyard
Superintendent of the Amsterdam
Admiralty (1725-1807).

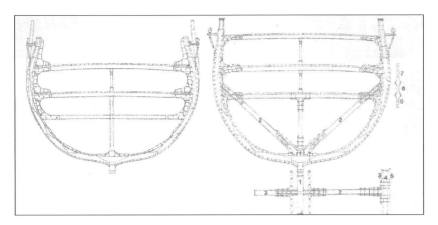

Comparative drawings of the midship sections of (left) a naval frigate of the late 18th C., and (right) one proposed by Gabriel Snodgrass. Robert Seppings system of strengthening the structure of the ship used riders, trusses, etc., between the frames, and all in the longitudinal plane. His system incorporated no extra cross-ship structural members. Snodgrass' proposed strengthening system, included the use of heavy diagonal braces in the transverse plane as illustrated. Explanatory key to Snodgrass diagram. 1. Keelson, 2. Diagonal brace, 3. Clamp, 4. Frame, 5. Hull planking, 6. Iron standard (not to scale), 7. Side arm, 8. Beam arm.

13 Portrait of John Milligen Seppings, Shipbuilder and Inspector of Shipping, East India Company at Calcutta. Son of Sir Robert Seppings.

14 Portrait of Marianne Seppings nee Matthews, m. John Milligen Seppings at Calcutta, 1823.

15 The framing of Seppings' Circular Stern, compared with the conventional Transom Stern.

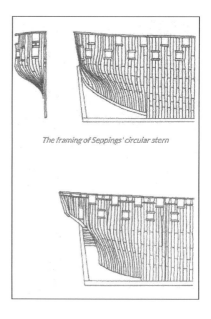

The framing of Seppings' circular stern

16 Portrait of Captain Edward James Seppings, H.E.I.C. Army, son of John Milligen and Marianne Seppings. Killed at the Massacre at Cawnpore. Grandson of Sir Robert Seppings.

17 Portrait of Lt. John Milligen Seppings R.N., Controller of Revenue Cutters. Sir Robert Seppings brother.

18 Engraving of the Danish-built ship Christian VII, showing the May-Hohlenberg pinched-in stern. After this ship was captured by the Royal Navy, British shipwrights found this style of stern both 'curious and interesting'.

19 HMS Victory.

20 HMS Victory under Jury Rig entering Gibraltar Bay after the Battle of Trafalgar.

21   HMS Unicorn preserved at Dundee.

22   Seppings' Iron Knees in HMS Unicorn.

23 & 24 Chatham No.3 Slipway, Seppings' Shed.

25 (opposite) Drawings of Seppings' Blocks.

The diagram marked *Fig 3* in the original document represents the adaption of Seppings Blocks used to strike topmasts.
Key: **a**, Top-gallant mast: **b**, Fid: **c**, Movable wedge: **d**, Trussel tree

Key to main diagram: **A**, Keelson: **B**, Ceiling: **C**, Floor timber: **D**, Dead or rising wood: **E**, Bottom planking: **F**, Keel and false keel: **G**, Angular blocks with a half-inch iron plate bolted to them: **H**, Cast-irin wedges: **I**, Iron plate of three-fourths of an inch thick on the bottom of the block: **K**, Battering-rams with wheels, and ropes for the hands: **L**, Cast-iron wedges, having received a blow from forward: **M**, Shores under the ship to sustain her weight.

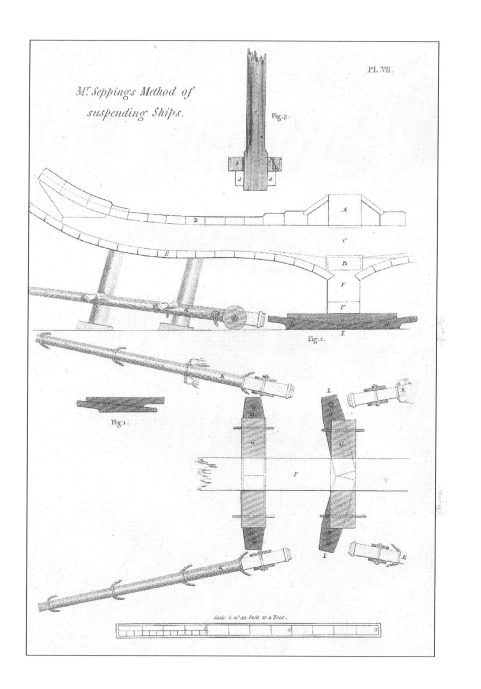

Mr. Sepping's Method of suspending Ships.

PL. VII.

Fig.3.

Fig.2.

Fig.1.

Scale ¼ of an Inch to a Foot.

26 The Fakenham Town sign.
   The depicted ship is in honour of
   Sir Robert Seppings.

27 One of the facsimile printer's
   blocks in Fakenham Market Place,
   honouring Sir Robert Seppings.

were shipped out for future use. They ended up at Woolwich Dockyard, where between June 1810 and February 1812 they were used in the construction of HMS *Chatham*. It turned out that the timbers were of such poor quality as to ensure that ship had a very short life indeed. By July 1814 she had become a Sheer Hulk at Chatham, and was condemned as unfit for even that non-seagoing purpose three years later. Possibly because of the strange way most of her timbers had been procured, there is no record of this ship's actual building cost in the Admiralty Progress Books. One can safely assume, however, that it was considerably more than the £5,110 that ship-breaker Joshua Crystall of Chatham paid for the hulk in 1817.

In 1816, Navy Board Comptroller Byam Martin, concerned about the eating away of Britain's strategic reserve of standing oak and acting after consultations with Robert Seppings, upgraded the efforts being made to find alternative supplies from abroad. The end of the war with France in 1815 meant that such oak markets as Dalmatia and Albania had reopened. On top of that, substitute hardwood sources were found within the Empire, including teak from India, iroko (known as 'poor man's teak') from Sierra Leone, and the aptly named stink-wood (*Ocotea bullata*) from South Africa, which has a highly unpleasant smell when newly felled, a smell that lingers even after the passage of months, even years. The 20-gun sloop HMS *Nimrod* launched in 1828 was built entirely of African timber. In 1832 – the last year of his tenure in office – Seppings ordered this ship to be thoroughly examined by the shipwrights at Plymouth and it was reported that she was 'dry, sound and without fungus'.

One practical problem that slowed up the conversion of felled timber into plank or board was the slowness of the old handsaw-cutting processes, and even of John Rennies' later water-powered sawmills. The steam-powered sawmill designed by Marc Isambard Brunel (Isambard Kingdom Brunel's father) significantly reduced this problem. Being more efficient, it also reduced the amount of wood wastage during conversion. The construction of Brunel's first steam sawmill together with some of its associated works began at Chatham in 1812 and was completed by the end of 1816. That period straddled the year 1813 in which Seppings was made Surveyor, and two stories, local to Chatham, concerning the relationship between him and Marc Brunel stem from that period, although neither of them is mentioned by Brunel's biographer.[49]

---

[49] Clements, *Marc Isambard Brunel.*

During the construction of the saw-mill's chimney, subsidence caused a problem that was rectified by Brunel designing iron-ties to help support it. The first of the two stories, implied that the faulty chimney was designed by Robert Seppings. No evidence has been found to support that claim, and as the project was entirely Brunel's brain-child it would seem very unlikely that Seppings had a direct role in designing any part of it.

The second story has it that Robert Seppings had Marc Brunel banned from entering Chatham Dockyard during the building of the mill. That Brunel was not in attendance at Chatham throughout the entire construction period is in fact borne out by some of the correspondence between him and the Navy Board in 1816, but there is nothing in that correspondence that points to any sort of ban. Early on Brunel had appointed a certain Mr. Ellicombe to superintend the ongoing works for him. By April 1816 those works had so progressed that, on the 23rd, the Navy Board wrote to Brunel asking his opinion on whether Ellicombe's services (for which the Board was paying) could now be dispensed with as 'we conceive that Mr. Brown the Master of the saw-mill, must now be fully competent to undertake the superintendence himself'.

In his reply dated 23 May, after stating that he had just arrived back from the Continent, Brunel went on:

> If at this period I am deprived of the services of Mr. Ellicombe to effect that which I have imparted to him during the gradual process of that undertaking, or in the course of correspondence that has subsisted between both him and myself, I should be under the necessity of making more frequent journeys to and from Chatham, a circumstance attended with great inconvenience to me and of greater expense to the public than Mr. Ellicombe's charges could possibly have been.

The consequence was that Mr. Ellicombe was retained for a time 'to be agreed with Mr. Brunel'.[50] Although this exchange does not specifically rule out the possibility that for some reason Brunel had been banned from entering the dockyard gates, it does rather imply that his non-attendance was simply because he was extremely busy elsewhere. (Brunel's biographer states that Brunel was fully occupied at Chatham in 1813, and in the following year was occupied in the building of a steam engine to be used in a packet-boat between London and Margate and in the rebuilding of his Battersea Veneer

[50] See file NMM CHA/F/29, at the National Maritime Museum.

Mill after it had been razed in a fire.) If, however, Brunel had been subject to some sort a banning order, it would not have been Seppings who imposed it. The overall administration of Royal Dockyards was never in the hands of the Surveyor, for each dockyard had an Admiralty Commissioner appointed to it who was a member of the Navy Board but resident locally, and it was he who was responsible for all matters pertaining to administration. The commissioner at Chatham from 1808 until 1823 was Captain (later Admiral Sir) Robert Barlow who resided within the dockyard at Commissioner's House. It would have been his decision, with the concurrence of the Navy Board of which Seppings was a member of course, to ban Brunel and issue the order. There appears now to be no record of any such ban, but if one was made, it is interesting to ask what might have been the cause of it and whether Sir Robert could have been involved in some sort of falling-out with Brunel. Brunel's plans for the world's first steam-driven sawmill were immense, and given that the mill was to be linked to the mast ponds by an underground canal and to timber storage areas by a mechanical transport system, and that the final product was to be used to build naval ships, there were plenty of opportunities for these two brilliant and strong-willed individuals to have clashed.

Another part of the timber problem was the proper management of timber seasoning. Most timbers used in shipbuilding did not have a long life. A number of factors were involved here including: the often inferior quality of the wood delivered by merchants in the first place; timber not being properly stored which led to dry and wet rot even, before the wood was even used; hasty construction in wartime that caused unseasoned timber to be used as a matter of course; great wastage in the use of the best timbers; and finally, because ships were built open to the weather at all stages of construction, and even after launching had to spend more months completely uncovered during the fitting out process, rain was able to infiltrate into every joint and cranny.

Always searching for ways to reduce timber wastage, around 1818 Seppings designed a system of laying deck planking diagonally instead of fore and aft, which meant that shorter planks in the form of cut-offs could be used, a change that significantly reduced wastage.

With regard to the storage problem, as early as 1806 when at Chatham, he had reported that most of the piled timber there was out in the open and stored in areas that were breeding grounds for fungi. That caused the Navy

Board to ask all yards to report on the condition of their piled stocks, and every one of them reported a similar sorry state of affairs.

An excellent example of the way he had of tackling problems head-on came when Seppings persuaded the Navy Board to allow him to scuttle a new ship that had just come off the blocks. In this eminently practical experiment, he set out to prove that salt water could cure dry rot. Very soon after the construction of the 20-gun sloop HMS *Eden* at William Courtney's yard at Chester in 1814 (she had cost around £12,000 to build, a considerable sum in those days), it was noticed that her oak timbers were already suffering from dry rot. So she was sailed round to Plymouth and there, in the protected waters of the Hamoaze (by then even more sheltered by the work being carried out on the construction of the Plymouth Breakwater), Seppings ordered her controlled scuttling on 9 November 1816. The ship lay underwater for four months before being raised on 12 March of the following year. Once the ship had dried out, an examination showed that the dry rot was entirely cured. From then on all new oak timbers completed their seasoning process in seawater, which entailed special measures involving tank vessels being used at riverside dockyards like those at Deptford and Woolwich where the river water was only brackish. (The *Eden* went on to have a relatively long working life. Commissioned in 1818, she then spent over twenty years in East Indian, West Indian, African and South American waters before finally being broken up in 1833.)

Sir Robert's work on battling wood-rot became well known and was often commented upon in the newspapers. In 1819 when Whigs and Tories were at hammer and tongs over some aspects of the British Constitution, an unnamed but learned wit, made reference to it in a rhyming simile under a quote in Latin by Cicero on the state of the Roman Republic.

> Tho' great is your praise, yet in vain have you hit on,
> A cure for the rot in the pride of each Briton.
> Unless you've some plan to effect restitution,
> By stopping *the rot* in our *old Constitution*. [51]

Copper-sheathing of a ship's hull below the waterline to protect it from the attentions of the wood-boring teredo worm, was first tried out in the British navy in 1761 on the frigate HMS *Alarm*. It was found to be satisfactory but only a few other ships were coppered because it was soon discovered that

---

[51] *Morning Chronicle*, London, 11 December 1819.

galvanic action between the copper sheets and the iron bolts that secured the hull planking to the frames, ate away at the iron. In 1783 after copper bolts were introduced, copper sheathing became general. However, over the years it was noted that corrosion of the copper was taking place, although it was not known until 1823 why that was so. It was the scientist Sir Humphry Davy who isolated the cause in that year when he was asked by the Navy Board (probably in the person of Robert Seppings, for the two had been acquainted with each other since at least December 1821, when according to London's *Morning Post* they both, in the company of the Marquess of Landsdowne, had attended a meeting of the Royal Society) to investigate the problem. He discovered that the corrosion was caused by electrical reaction between the copper and the oxygenated seawater stirred up by the ship's motion through the water. He reasoned that if the electrical polarity between the copper and the seawater could be reversed, creation of the corrosive copper salts would cease. In the first application of what he called 'cathodic protection', he used iron anodes because iron was much more electro-positive than copper. In February of the following year, Sir Humphry's anodes, called 'protectors' were fixed to the bottom of the copper-sheathed cutter HMS *Surly* at Portsmouth in the presence of both the inventor and Robert Seppings. (This pairing caused one newspaper editor to quip that, 'Sir Humphry Davy was concerned with ships' bottoms, like Sir Robert Seppings was concerned with ships' knees'.) For the next two months *Surly* was monitored closely (one of the observers being the scientist Michael Faraday), and satisfied that the test had been successful, the Navy Board then drafted an order for all ships to be so fitted. Unfortunately, Davy's invention had an unintended consequence. In 1825 it was found that because the protectors had eliminated the production of copper salts, ships' bottoms were more quickly becoming fouled by seaweed and barnacles to which those salts had been poisonous. So the original order was rescinded. It has been said that despair over this failure contributed to Davy's early death in 1829. (His experiments came into their own later in the century however, when iron hulls superseded wood, and when propellers were introduced. It was found that zinc anodes protected the iron hull against the local galvanic effects caused by the presence of a turning bronze propeller.)

In a report to the Admiralty in January 1830, Seppings described 'a method of roofing ships over when under construction', but it was not until 1838, six years after he had left the Admiralty, that a permanent structure, the No. 3 Covered Slip, was built at Chatham to his design. With its awe-inspiring cantilever roof, it was described at the time as being at the cusp of technological change, and was in fact the largest wide-span timber structure in Europe. The shed, now named after Seppings, with its in excess of 400 windows, still stands although its purpose has changed. Any person standing inside and looking up at the massive curve of its roof and its struts and tresses, might be tempted to regard it as an upside down version of one of his ships, though it is of course, nothing of the sort.

Robert Seppings was by no means the first to advocate the practice of covering slips and docks to keep the rain out during construction. We have seen that Gabriel Snodgrass had advocated this in 1771, and there had been others before that date and since, including Sir Jeremy Bentham, who until 1812 had been the navy's Inspector-General of Naval Works responsible for the maintenance of the Dockyards. No doubt Bentham's ideas influenced those of Seppings, who indeed, whilst still Master Shipwright at Chatham in 1812 and superintending the building of HMS *Howe*, had been instructed to roof over that ship (with a temporary structure that apparently included the use of oiled paper as windows) during construction, and also to roof over the piles of stored timber during the seasoning process.[52] Since becoming Surveyor he had battled continuously to find funds to roof over all timber stocks (which in the case of most yards also meant purchasing or leasing extra land on which to do it), and to roof over some of the building slips. Lack of funds ensured that progress was slow, and often the device of using temporary roofs over slips and docks was resorted to. It has been reported that 'at least 36 temporary roofs spread around Woolwich, Chatham, Portsmouth, Devonport, Sheerness, Pembroke and Deptford', were constructed by Seppings.[53] He also conducted experiments in roofing over ships lying in ordinary, and thankfully we can all still enjoy one result of his labours in that direction when we look at the frigate HMS *Unicorn* built at Chatham in 1824 and now preserved at Dundee.

John Knowles, Clerk of Surveyors under Seppings, and his friend, gave Plymouth and 1814 (rather than Chatham and 1812 as above) as the place and date for Seppings' first temporary slip-way roof. Knowles first wrote to this effect in a Supplement to the Encyclopaedia Britannica, which caused a certain Mr. Richard Pering to write to London's *Morning Chronicle* on 14 November 1820, to claim that the idea and plans for that slip-way roof were his, not Seppings. John Knowles replied in that paper's next edition,

---

[52] Packard papers.
[53] Skempton, *Biographical Dictionary of Civil Engineers*.

stating that Pering, the Admiralty Clerk of the Check at Plymouth, had indeed submitted plans for such a roof but they had not been accepted and implied that Pering being 'only an accountant', could hardly have expected otherwise. The 9 December edition of that paper carried another letter from Pering in which he made the specific point that a part of his plan dealing with projecting eaves, 'had found their way into the plans of Sir Robert Seppings'. For some reason this row by open correspondence did not develop further; mayhap the newspaper's editor drew a line under it. But it does show that Sir Robert Seppings was continuing to be a person of controversy.

Teak as a timber for shipbuilding has been mentioned several times in this work, not least when discussing the career of Sir Robert's son. It seems worthwhile to discuss this timber in a little more detail and explain why more ships were not built of it.

For centuries teak (tectona grandis) has been regarded as the very best timber for building ships on account of what have been called 'its noble qualities'. These include long-term durability, high strength and stiffness, the absence of cracks and splits in any artefact made from it, its high resistance to rot, fungi and mildew, and due to its natural oils, its high resistance to termites and other pests.

Teak grew mainly in India, Burma and in parts of the East Indies, and local sailing craft had been built from it in those countries for centuries prior to the penetration of the Indian sub-continent and parts of South East Asia by Europeans. According to Professor C.R. Boxer, 'The superiority of Indian teak over European pine and oak for shipbuilding purposes was early recognized' by the Portuguese, the first Europeans to reach India by sea.[54] Boxer went on to quote a Portuguese royal order of 1585 that stated it would be preferable for ships engaged in the trade between the sub-continent and Portugal to be built in India, because they lasted longer than home-built ones, were cheaper to build, and because suitable timber was becoming increasingly hard to find at home. That order was largely ignored mainly because of the strategic necessity of keeping the shipbuilding yards in Portugal busy. The same strategic consideration applied when later the Dutch, the French and the British muscled in on the Eastern trade. Every European maritime nation had to keep its domestic shipbuilding yards, which during the 17th and 18th centuries formed the larger part of all its industrial undertakings, viable and

[54] Boxer, C.R., *The Portuguese Seaborne Empire, 1415-1825.*

busy and available for the repair and dry-docking of ships, as well as the building of them. In addition, there was the benefit that home yards were under direct and immediate domestic control. So, although some European countries including Britain, did build ships in India and other parts of the East, the numbers were small in comparison with home-built ones. And of course, transporting teak all the way home in anything other than the smallest quantities, would not have been an attractive alternative to the many other more commercially valuable cargoes available for ships engaged in the Eastern Trade.

There may well have been other reasons for not relying too much on Indian shipyards. Joseph Cotton (1745-1825), one-time mariner before becoming an influential director of the Hon. East India Company, writing in 1799, contended that:

> 'Ships of Force should be admitted only in the Company's Employ, and the Pre-eminence in Naval Strength ought to be European. If vessels are built in any Number, or navigated by the Natives, the Tendency cannot but be alarming. Imperceptible are the Steps from Weakness to Power, from Restraint to Independence.'[55]

Cotton was mostly concerned about the building of ships in India to be used in what was known as the 'Country Trade', the coastal trade between Indian ports and from those ports to China – opium clippers, for example, some of which were owned or part owned by Indian traders. In general, they were better built even than the home-built, high quality East Indiamen that traded directly between Europe and India and the Far East. He was worried lest the HEIC's monopolistic control of trades with India and China be affected. But, of course, there were wider connotations to his statement, than just that.

Like all other European shipbuilders, Sir Robert Seppings was well aware of the benefits of teak. He, no doubt, would also have had the opportunity of reading his son's treatise on the subject. He once wrote, 'Teak is the most durable [of woods], but differs very much in quality'. He went on to designate Malabar Northern Teak as the most valuable timber in the world for shipbuilding.[56] One supposes that he must often have rued the fact that the source of teak was not nearer home.

---

[55] Quoted by C. Northcote Parkinson in *The Trade Winds*.
[56] See, Walker, F.M., *Ships and Shipbuilders: Pioneers of Designs & Constructions*.

Whilst reading the above résumé of Seppings and the timber problem, the reader might well have asked himself why, because of the timber shortage, more use was not made of iron and especially iron knees, much, much earlier than it was? The answer is several-fold. Tradition was perhaps at the heart of it, for shipwrights were always a mighty conservative bunch and up to the arrival on the scene of Byam Martin, so were most Naval Board members; in fact throughout the Navy, save for a few imaginative pioneers like Seppings, there was a wide-spread and obstinate opposition to innovation combined with an utter contempt for any kind of scientific learning.

Private cupidity also played its role – some might even say the major role – in keeping wood in and iron out. Many influential officials in government, in the navy itself, and elsewhere in power, had invested in one way or another in the lucrative timber trade and so were not about to support the use of any other kind of material. (Many of the nation's oak forests and groves were on estates owned by powerful landowners.)

Then there was the matter of the iron itself. Wrought iron was expensive and early on was full of impurities and so likely to fracture. New processes had improved the quality by the time Snodgrass began using his iron knees in HEIC ships, but that was still not proof enough to make the navy change its mind in any major sort of way. Foundries and Smithies had been in place at most dockyards for many years producing anchors, bolts and nails and, more recently, the copper sheeting required for hull sheathing. As time went on and the navy's stance on iron eased a little, the increasing use of iron in ships led to a demand for larger and improved iron-working facilities (at Chatham for example, the so-called No.1 Smithery was built in 1801), but that all cost money which often was not available.

A common excuse was that iron rusts, and at that time there was no really efficient coating to prevent this. The use of improperly seasoned timber, of course, raised the risk of rust in any iron fittings that were in contact with that wood.

Change did come, but very slowly. By the time HMS *Trincomalee* came to be built in India in 1817, Seppings' design of iron plate knees associated with wooden chocks had become more-or-less standard practice. Some of these can still be seen in that ship at Hartlepool. They can also be seen in HMS *Unicorn* at Dundee.

It must have been at some time in the early 1820s (internal evidence shows that it was post 1819 the year in which Sir Robert was knighted) that Rear Admiral Byam Martin felt it right and proper that his friend and colleague should reap some financial benefit from the many inventions and improvements he had made since receiving that bonus for improving dry-dock technology. Byam Martin's undated letter addressed to Lord Liverpool, Premier and First Lord of the Treasury, gives an indication of the great sums of money Seppings' many changes had saved the nation, and for that reason it is quoted at length here.[57] It went:

> "The advantage which the public service has derived from the various inventions of Sir Robert Seppings have already been detailed and constitute a fair claim for reward proportionate in some degree to the annual saving which they effect; but as the smallest percentage founded upon such data would amount to a very large sum, I beg permission to point out the reasonableness of rewarding his long, anxious, and laborious efforts in carrying into effect and perfecting those inventions, by taking one of them as a standard for reward, and for this purpose I would submit that his new method of timbering ships be alone considered. By this system small timber can be applied as a substitute for large and generally speaking may be used for purposes to which it was not before considered applicable: thus the delay and difficulty of procuring what was termed 'construction timber' is completely obviated, as every part of the frame may now be obtained from the common store, without having to await as heretofore years for timber to complete the frames, by which trees of the falls of various years have been put into the same ship; besides which, this principle of building greatly increases the strength and durability of the fabric. Without however calculating upon the vast saving which must arise from the longer period the ships will last, I will merely beg to offer for consideration the following facts:

---

[57] In the Liverpool Papers Ms.38.368 held in the British Library and quoted here with permission.

			£
Saving in timbering a Ship of the Line on two decks			2,000
,,	a Frigate of 60 guns		1,600
,,	,,	46 & 42 guns	500
,,	,,	28 ,,	200

There are now building and ordered to be built upon this principle:

			£
Ships of Line		24 at £2,000	48,000
Frigates of 60 guns		6 at 1,600	9,600
,,	48 & 46 guns	30 at 500	15,000
,,	28 guns	15 at 200	3,000
		Total	**£ 75,600**

Byam Martin then went on:

"If then 1/7 only of the savings on the ships *building* and *ordered* were given, it would amount to a sum exceeding £10,000.

It has been said that the Government has a right to the abilities and exertions of those who hold official situations: granting this to the fullest extent, it surely cannot be maintained that a person is to apply his ingenuity to the accomplishment of great national objects, sacrifice the usual hours of leisure, in preparing designs and digesting instructions for the execution of his plans (some of which are not attached even to his own profession), injure his health by unremitting assiduity in such pursuits, and voluntarily take upon himself a heavy responsibility, not required of him by his office, and encounter and triumph over the jealousy and prejudice of professional men, without obtaining some adequate reward for important services, which can but be considered as extraordinary and distinct from the duties required of him. In making the aforementioned statement I have not in any way considered that material improvement in building ships on the diagonal system (which may be considered an era in shipbuilding) nor many others whence great savings have arisen, altho' of a minor description, which have been invented and introduced by Sir R. Seppings. Upon the fact of giving rewards to persons in office for inventions connected with their profession, I am prepared to state several instances if required to do so; perhaps it may be sufficient to say that Colonel Shrapnel has long been in the enjoyment of £100 per annum for his shells which have scarcely ever been used."

Lord Liverpool did not act upon the Comptroller's recommendations. It is likely that the cost of rewarding the genius of Seppings in some monetary way, even in the watered-down way suggested, was considered prohibitive and might well have opened the door for other government servants demanding similar treatment.

7
Steam ships and Experimental Squadrons

The end of the Napoleonic Wars in 1815 brought about a renaissance in European interest in the exploration of the interior of Africa. Of especial interest was the course of the River Niger and its relation to that of the River Congo. Britain's War Department put forward the idea that the Congo should be explored to see if there was any sort of confluence with the Niger, and it was thought that any such riverine expedition was best suited as a naval venture. Admiralty Secretary Sir John Barrow became interested in it and proceeded to get Sir Joseph Banks' support, 'on the premise that nothing could be done without his active engagement'.[58] The construction of a steam-driven, paddle-wheeled vessel became central to the plan, and for that Sir Robert Seppings was brought in. (As Barrow, like Banks and Seppings, was also an FRS, the fingers of knightly fellows were all over this venture.)

James Watt junior, advised the Admiralty that an engine of not less than 20 horsepower would be required to face the expected Congo currents and that such a machine just happened to be building at the family firm of Boulton & Watts for the Tyne Packet Company. Banks called in John Rennie (adding another to the list of FRSs involved) on the question of the engine and the performance required of it, and received confirmation of Watt's advice. So in August 1815 Seppings began working on the design of the *Congo*, the first paddle steamer ever built to Admiralty order. (As it turned out - see below - the *Congo* was never commissioned into the navy in that capacity, so the honour of being the first naval paddle steamer is now bestowed upon HMS *Comet* built in 1822, also to a design of Seppings, assisted in that case by Oliver Lang, the Master Shipwright at Woolwich.)

The *Congo* of 100-tons, was to draw no more than 4 feet. The vessel had to be stable enough to sail down the Atlantic Ocean to the mouth of the Congo, and then be capable of sailing up the river after which she was named which was known to have long stretches of shallow narrows in it through which the water ran very swiftly indeed. The engine to be used

[58] Carter, *Sir Joseph Banks*, p. 498.

weighed 30 tons and was 20 feet wide and took up the complete breadth of the ship when completed. Some of the requirements proved technically incompatible, and on top of that, the ship was designed to fit the engine rather than the other way round. The *Congo* was launched at Deptford Dockyard at the end of January 1816, and her trials showed that on a consumption of three tons of wood fuel a day (the only fuel available where she was going), her best rate of speed was only five-and-a-half knots at a working draft of 4 feet 3 inches. That speed was considered too low to stem the Congo currents, and the draft was considered too deep. In consequence the engine was removed and the ship was then commissioned into the navy as the three-masted schooner-rigged HMS *Congo*.[59] After being fitted with three sliding keels for stability at sea she did sail for the River Congo. (She spent the rest her life as a surveying vessel and was sold to shipbreakers in 1826.)

Naval Paddle-Steamers designed wholly or in part by Sir Robert Seppings

	Tons	Launched
Comet	240	Deptford 23 May 1822 (Oliver Lang assisted in this design.)
Lightning	296	Deptford 19 September 1823
Meteor	296	Deptford 17 February 1824
African	295	Woolwich 30 August 1825
Alban	294	Deptford 27 December 1826
Carron	294	Deptford 9 January 1827
Confiance	295	Woolwich 28 March 1827
Echo	295	Woolwich 28 May 1827
Columbia	361	Woolwich 1 July 1829
Phoenix	809	Chatham 25 September 1832
Dee	704	Woolwich 25 March 1834

Notes.   a) The last two were launched after Seppings' retirement.

b) All had successful careers, some ending their days as naval tugs.

c) Seppings' original plans for both the *African* and the *Dee* were recorded as 'adjusted by Oliver Lang'.

No blame attached to Seppings for the *Congo* business and he went on to design several other steam-driven vessels without the handicap of having to work within incompatible specifications. (See table above.)

_____

[59] It is reported that the *Congo* engine was later used for pumping out the Royal Docks at Plymouth.

Because steam-driven vessels did not have to await favourable winds in order to sail and were far more comfortable than long inland coach journeys, from the start of their appearance in the navy they tended to be used by senior Admiralty officials for their regular visitations to ports and dockyards. Seppings and Byam Martin made several such voyages in HMS *Comet*, and on one of them were accompanied by royalty. In July 1827 the Lord High Admiral, H.R.H. the Duke of Clarence, made such a tour to some of the west coast ports. Also on board were the Duchess of Clarence, Miss Fitzclarence, and Princess Carlotti of Saxe Meiningen (the Duchess's cousin). The ship also carried the Lord High Admiral's large retinue. Temporary additional accommodation was erected on deck, but even so the ship must have been rather crowded. Anyway, the ladies left the steamer at Tenby, 'to return home by land'. The remainder of the party went on to visit Pembroke Dockyard in Milford Haven, and then sailed round to Bristol.

The use of Seppings diagonal system and his other improvements soon spread worldwide, with navies and merchant shipping companies everywhere taking up his ideas. It has already been mentioned that the Kyd dockyard in Calcutta used his system in the building of the *Warren Hastings* in 1819. Two years later the Wadia Yard in Bombay launched the 80-gun HMS *Ganges* also built to his principles. (The stern of this ship did not have the Seppings' pinched-in stern, although later ships in the same class did.)[60]

During his lifetime some of Seppings' critics accused him of building heavy ships. Heavy sailing ships lacked in sailing qualities and so of course, tended to be comparatively slow, and it was mainly over this factor that the criticisms arose. The critics highlighted the fact that the French now had many ships that were faster than their British equivalents, but failed to mention that the French were now building their ships using the Seppings' system. In fact the 'heavy ship' criticism, although it may have been true when his stiffening arrangements were added to existing vessels, was probably not true in the case of new ships built to his system. Seppings once claimed that there was a considerable reduction in the number of trees needed to build a ship when

---

[60] *Ganges* was the very last sailing vessel of the Royal Navy to sail as an Admiral's flagship; in the Pacific from 1857 to 1861 when based at Valparaiso. However, she is chiefly remembered by generations of naval trainees for being a naval training ship firstly at Falmouth in 1865, then as part of the Royal Navy Training Establishment at Shotley, Suffolk from 1900, an establishment that later came to be named after her. This teak-built, grand old lady lasted for 109 years before being broken up at Plymouth in 1930.

his methods were used, and according to naval architect David K. Brown, 'that must have equated to a weight reduction'.[61] Nevertheless, in the early 1820s these 'heavy-ship' criticisms, mainly from serving officers of the navy, increased in tempo and questions on the subject were being asked in both Houses of Parliament. (It must be mentioned that many of these criticisms suffered from political bias, not so much directly from the various protagonists, but from their backers in Parliament. Most members of the Navy Board at this time were Tories, and the backers of his loudest critic, Captain William Symonds, were Whigs. There seems to be little in the way of evidence indicating Seppings' political inclinations but, as most of his friends including Comptroller Byam Martin were die-hard Tories, it seems likely that his political leanings were also in that direction.)

In the face of this fire from many directions the Admiralty decided to organise what came to be called the first and second experimental squadrons to test the sailing abilities of the ships involved. Most of the ships that took part were specially designed for the purpose, and most were 18-gun sloops. Some were built to designs of the two principal naval detractors of the status quo, Captains William Symonds and John Hayes. One of Symonds' ships was the *Columbine* built at Portsmouth in 1826, and one of Hayes' called *Champion* was built in 1824. Three, the *Orestes*, *Sapphire* and *Fly* were built to the designs of Doctor Inman of the School of Naval Architecture. Three were designed by Sir Robert Seppings, namely the *Acorn* built at Chatham, the *Satellite* at Pembroke Dock, both in 1826, and *Pylades* built at Woolwich in 1824. His 28-gun frigate *Tyne* built at that last place in 1826 was also in attendance during the trials. The experimental cruises took place in the Channel and out as far as the Scilly Islands, between May and late October 1827, and the squadrons involved were under the command of Rear Admiral Sir Thomas Hardy (Nelson's flag captain in HMS *Victory*) flying his flag firstly in *Sybille* and then in *Pyramus*, both 28-gun frigates and both prizes taken from the French which were almost certainly included in the squadron for comparative purposes.

The following description of these squadrons has been pieced together from newspaper reports and from articles and letters that appeared in learned journals at the time. Most of the commentators concerned used the premise that the trials, which were mainly in the form of races, were between vessels designed by three distinct schools of thought, namely the new scientific

---

[61] Seppings entry, *DNB*, 2nd edition.

methodology of shipbuilding as taught by Doctor Inman in his school, the empirical system based on the sailing experiences and experiments of serving naval officers, and lastly the shipwrights whose training was largely based on passed down rule-of-thumb technology. That premise, however, was very much an over-simplification. Captain Symonds for example, had devoted much of the period he spent as captain of the port of Malta between 1819 and 1825, in studying ship construction at the naval repair yard there which was run by shipwrights trained in the old ways. Captain (later Rear Admiral) Hayes had an even closer relationship with those old methods. His father George had been a Master Boat Builder at a commercial yard near Deptford, and his great-uncle Adam Hayes was once Master Shipwright at the Royal Deptford Dockyard and had there taken his great nephew under his wing for a number of years before the young man joined his first ship HMS *Orion* as a midshipman in 1787. Furthermore, no one can say that Sir Robert Seppings, trained in the old ways as he was, had not brought in innovations based on experimentation, or that his approach to many of these matters was unscientific. Something else to consider was that, like every other Surveyor before him, he was always financially-constrained by the size of the Naval Estimates periodically voted on by Parliament, and that the ships specifically built for the experimental voyages appear not to have been cost-constrained in the same strict way. (For one thing, the speed at which some of these ships were built indicates that shipwrights involved must have worked overtime, which was expensive.) That having been said, Seppings acting under orders from the Navy Board, did control the expenditure on these ships to some extent by issuing a maximum tonnage parameter, which could not be exceeded. (In the case of one of the ships involved there seems to have been a particularly strict and highly unusual financial arrangement. In 1824 His Grace the 4th Duke of Portland, who had a dilettante's interest in shipbuilding and naval design, managed to persuade the Admiralty to permit the construction of an 18-gun sloop at Portsmouth – possibly HMS *Champion* – 'under an unusual and restrictive penalty' arrangement underwritten by the Duke. One assumes this meant that had the vessel not met certain laid-down conditions of excellence during her trials, His Grace would have had to pay for the ship. The ship was built with a wider beam than usual to give greater stability, and with a sharper, wedge-like bottom to give her more speed. Her trials held in early 1825, proved a success.)

Of all the ships involved in these trials the one of most interest to us is the *Satellite*, for not only was that ship designed by Seppings, he also spent a number of weeks at Pembroke personally overseeing her construction. (This was the year, 1826, in which his brother John Milligen Seppings died at Chudleigh in Devon: it is not known whether Seppings was able to attend the funeral, but as they had always been close it is likely that he did.)

An edition of London's *Morning Post* in July of that year noted that, 'Sir Robert Seppings is still at Pembroke Dock', where the *Satellite* was building; and he was still there at her launching on 7 October. That same newspaper's edition for 11 October, announced:

'*Launch of the Satellite, Milford Haven, October 7.*

The Satellite experiment ship of 18 guns constructed by Sir Robert Seppings, Surveyor of the Navy and intended to sail against those built on the plans of Capt. Hay[es] R.N. was launched this week from Pembroke Dockyard. Although the season for such amusements has far advanced, yet the novelty of the ship and the mildness of the weather, attracted a number of natives to the spot. She has a very handsome bottom and was only twelve weeks in building from first to last. Captain John Laws R.N., a nephew of Sir Robert, had the honour of naming her. She has been decked, coppered and rigged and will sail for Plymouth, the first favourable wind.'

Commander John Milligen Laws (he was not made post-captain until 7 January 1833) who launched the ship, was also to be her first captain. He was in command when she took part in the experimental cruises, and remained in command afterwards when she sailed for Indian waters on a surveying voyage.

> **The Laws Connection.**
>
> Lydia, Robert Sepping's eldest sister who had been adopted by Captain and Mrs. John Milligen in 1780 and who had returned home to Fakenham in about 1787 when aged 25, was married twice: firstly, to William Sampson of nearby Rudham and they had one daughter called Anne.
>
> After Sampson's death in 1790 Lydia married a saddler called Mr. Green Laws of Fakenham. By him she had three daughters and three sons. All three sons received considerable help from Seppings at the commencement of what proved to be three successful navy-connected careers. The importance of 'interest' in the Navy has already been mentioned and Robert's use of it to help his Laws nephews provides us with good examples.

The eldest son Edward Laws born in 1791, was found a post in the administrative side of the Admiralty. He was Naval Storekeeper at Quebec and then, in 1814, held a similar position at Kingston, Ontario. By 1820 he was holding the very important post of Clerk of the Cheque at Pembroke Dock, a position he held for many years. On retirement he became mayor of the town, and Laws Street there is named after him. He died in 1854. (His son, also Edward, was the author of the celebrated book, *The History of Little England Beyond Wales*.)

The second son Robert Laws (1798-1889) was taken on as an extra clerk in Sepping's office at Chatham and moved with him to London and so would have served under Chief Clerk John Knowles. Robert ended his career in a senior position at Plymouth Dockyard.

The youngest son John Milligen Laws was born in 1799. In 1810 Robert Seppings persuaded Commander Nicolas Lockyer to take the 11-year old John into HM sloop *Sophie* as a Volunteer 1st Class – an unpaid budding Midshipman – whom he would have had to support. (This Lockyer was the brother of Ann Lockyer who had married Robert's brother John in 1804.) The by then Rear Admiral Laws died in 1859.

All three Laws boys were remembered in Sir Robert Seppings' will.

The launching of the *Satellite* turned out to be something of a family affair. As well as Sir Robert Seppings and Commander Laws, Edward Laws, Clerk of the Cheque and Receiver of Stores, was also in attendance. He lived with his family at No. 2 The Terrace in the Dockyard, a row of houses in which all the yard's Principal Officers resided. (The Captain Superintendent would have lived at No.1.) As all the evidence indicates that the Seppings' were always a close-knit family, it is very likely that Sir Robert's invalid son Andrew, who lived with a surgeon only a few miles away, was also there. On top of all that, Lamphey Court the seat of a certain Charles Mathias Esq. whose family fortune had been made from plantations in Jamaica, lay not too far away from the dockyard, and as one of the foremost local dignitaries he was most likely in attendance too. But be that as it may, within ten years his only daughter Mary Mathias had married the by then Captain John Milligen Laws. (They had two sons.)

Sir Robert's lengthy stay at Pembroke Dock shows he had taken very particular care over the building and fitting out of the *Satellite*. Also, in view of the fact the ship was specially constructed to take part in the experimental squadrons and that his reputation was at least partly at stake, he must have held a high opinion of his 27-year old nephew's ship-handling skills.

As it turned out, the experimental trials were not considered a success by most neutral commentators. In an article under the heading '*Observations on the State of Naval Construction in this Country*',[62] one of those commentators wrote:

> It is with regret that we must conclude upon careful consideration that although the experiments are carried on with much vigour and interest, they are evidently founded on imaginative views and that there cannot exist anything like legitimate data where so many failures and anomalous results obtain. Who can read the account of the experimental squadron without immediately perceiving that the constructors of the contending vessels, however sanguine each might have been of his particular fancy, met with nothing but the most perplexing results? We see that sometimes one and sometimes the other vessel claim the palm of excellence, and finally leaving the subject as much in the dark as ever…

He went on:

> We cannot refrain here from noticing the paucity of information contained in the reports hitherto made on the first Experimental Squadron. The best one is but little removed from a ship's log book, and in some respects is inferior to it: it is of such scanty nature, that we can scarcely inform ourselves on any point, and that only in a *relative* degree, of the qualities of the vessels composing it; we cannot find any mention of their *absolute* velocities on the different points of sailing, which is a most important omission. We are neither informed in what way the observations were conducted, whether they were made simultaneously or not: unless the former, any attempt at comparison must be very doubtful, if not entirely fallacious. Circumstances of wind and weather may very widely and alter in the course of a short time, and every endeavour at legitimate analogy be destroyed by such variation.

That commentator also expressed his distress that the reports presented only a rough idea of the strength of the winds because the observers were using the numbers on the Beaufort scale. Those 'Forces' were adequate enough for standard nautical and meteorological purposes, but not during what

---

[62] *Quarterly Journal of Science, Literature and Art,* July/December 1827, London.

were supposed to be scientific experiments. (Beaufort's Force 5 for example, covered the range of wind speeds 17 to 21 knots.) An anemometer giving precise speeds should have been used he maintained. He especially criticised 'the learned professor Dr. Inman' for not ascertaining the centre of gravity point of any of his ships, by the 'very principles he taught in his school'. He went on 'The knowledge of the position of that point would have placed him so far head of his competitors....that we are surprised he should have thrown away this advantage and descended to a level with his less scientific opponents'.

In his drubbing of the experiments, that commentator could also have mentioned that the relative skills and experience of the various commanders involved was an important factor. Some shiphandlers liked a certain rake to the masts in particular wind conditions; some had a penchant for lessening or increasing the tension on the stays. As most sailing ships sail better in a slightly down-by-the-head configuration, the captain's preferred degree was achieved by moving ballast, and that preferred degree differed between captains. On top of all that, some captains were habitual risk takers, others were always more cautious. How does one go about measuring and comparing those factors?

A writer in another learned journal came to similar conclusions about the results before going off on a different tack to take a swipe at Dr. Inman's school.[63]

> The experimental squadrons that have left us with a multitude of perplexing results, have elicited it must be confessed, an interesting fact, viz. that there has been an establishment, seventeen years in this country in Portsmouth Dockyard for the scientific education of the naval architects for the Royal Navy. With respect to ourselves we see nothing interesting in the fact of the country being burdened with the expense of a college (whether for the scientific education of naval architects or students of any other side of science) for the past seventeen years without it being clearly shown that the country has a reasonable hope of a fair return for its bounty and expense.

That writer had probably learned that students from that school had been appointed to accompany at least some of the ships of the squadron, and

---

[63] *Neptune Magazine* of 1828.

clearly thought that the results should therefore have been much less perplexing than he found them to be.[64]

The anonymous author of a pamphlet called *Remarks on the Conduct of the Naval Administration of Great Britain since 1815 by a Flag Officer* published early in 1830 stated that during the experiments, 'The *Champion* and *Orestes* were both superior ships to Sir Robert Seppings' *Pylades*, and possessed many good qualities of stability and stowage which the latter wanted'. That caused the Surveyor's heckles to rise. In a letter to the editor of the *United Services Journal*, Seppings wrote after quoting those words of 'Flag Officer':

> Let us revert on this subject to the official report of Capt. Sturt, who commanded the operations of the squadron at the final cruise of their trial, in refutation of this, who says, 'The *Pylades* has gained much celebrity, and is most certainly entitled to be placed first on the list of this cruise, when sailing on a wind. She carries her canvass [sic] in an astonishing way, and in spite of wind and sea, creeps away to windward like a clipper... She certainly has very great Weatherly qualities, and is particularly stiff under her canvass.[65]

Seppings went on,

> But if further evidence be necessary of her good qualities, Capt. Jackson, who subsequently commanded the *Pylades*, says, 'She stows three months provisions very well, stands up under sail, steers, wears, and stays, remarkably well. She is very weatherly, never having seen anything to equal her in this property, and she has beaten every vessel she has fallen in with'; and these are the observations of the captain after an experience of several years.

The anonymous 'Flag Officer' had also made this criticism of Seppings. "The first great mistake committed, appeared to be in limiting the constructors unnecessarily as to dimensions, and more especially as to the breadth of their ships, by insisting that they were not to exceed a certain prescribed tonnage." In reply, Seppings wrote:

---

[64] The name of one of those accompanying students is known. Called Chatfield, he had invented what he called a *nauropometer*, a device to measure a ship's inclination, 'which exhibits the angles of pitching and rolling at one view'. It consisted of two graduated semicircles set at right angles to each other, one of which was on gimbals, whilst the other had to be fixed to the ship's structure. It is not recorded whether Chatfield actually carried one with him during the experiments. (See *Niles' Register* for 28 August 1828.)

[65] *U.S.J.*, 1830, Part 3, p. 228.

This, however, as far as breadth is concerned, was not the fact. But everyone who is conversant with naval architecture knows, that where limits are prescribed, the genius and talents of the best architect… will be better shown when he is left with regard to dimensions to the exercise of his own discretion; and it is a fact which cannot be controverted, that in point of expense, whether considered in reference to the building and first equipment, or in reference to the subsequent wear and tear of the hulls of ships and their stores, the smaller they are to carry the number of guns prescribed and to secure the necessary sea-going qualities, the more advantageous they will be to a country. The constructors were not limited either to form, length or breadth, the only limitation was…they should not exceed a prescribed tonnage. In this it will be seen that they were not cramped with regard to dimensions, for the 28-gun ships were allowed to be one hundred tons larger than ships of the class then in the Navy, which had answered very well; and some of the corvettes (the *Columbine* for instance) are one hundred and ten tons larger than the 18-gun brigs, a class of vessels which the writer praises, although each class is armed with the same number and nature of ordnance. And so far from there being an 'invincible unwillingness' on my part to increase the breadth of ships, I have done this, in most classes of ships, to a greater extent than was ever before practised in the British Navy.

He went on to elaborate on the association of breadth with stability-

That an increase in breadth gives a great increase of stability when ships are planned by an able constructor, is not to be denied but it is not this only which produces that quality, for there are several other considerations. Thus, the advantage of increased breadth may be lost by mal-construction, and a disadvantage arise from it, that of increased resistance [through the water], when the theory of ship-building is not thoroughly understood by a person who plans a draught. Besides, there are cases where too much stability is an evil rather than an advantage. But it is unnecessary for me to carry this reasoning farther in refutations of assertions by the author of the pamphlet, who has proved himself ignorant even of the elements of Naval Architecture.

The anonymous 'Flag Officer' author of the pamplet had also gone on to criticise HMS *Tyne*'s performance during the sailing trials. Sir Robert excused that ship's apparent failure by alluding to the fact that any ship's sailing qualities 'are dependent upon the skill and activity of the Commander'. He went on,

'It was unfortunate for the credit of this ship that her Captain, during the greater part of the trial of sailing, was laid upon the bed of sickness which indisposition has since terminated in death: this no doubt was the principal cause of her apparent failure'. (Both he and the author of the pamphlet failed to mention that during the trials off Scilly on 25 September 1827, with a strong wind blowing, the *Tyne* was in collision with the *Neptunus*, a Swedish timber ship, and was 'obliged to put back to Portsmouth for repairs'.)

Sir Robert then went on to support his claim that had the captain of the *Tyne* been fit then the ship's performance might have been judged better, by reporting 'the character of this ship during the last three years while under the command of Capt. Sir Richard Grant – it is this: "The Tyne steers easy, wears and stays well, rides well at her anchors, and stands very well under her sails, so much so, that it was judged right to land twenty-five tons of ballast, as she is an excellent sea-boat. In a tremendous gale of wind she was found to be easy, and shipped little or no water." '

The Surveyor then told us something about the overall principle on which all of his work had been based.

> My principle has ever been to construct and mast ships of war for
> general purposes, and not to suit a particular occasion, so that they
> may possess good sea-going properties under all the variations of wind
> and weather; how far I have succeeded in this, in the ships which made
> up part of the Experimental Squadron, I shall leave to the judgement
> of your readers, after a perusal of these reports.
> There is, however, one point on which I have reason to complain of a
> want of fairness and candour in the author, it is this – he states that,
> "Two 18-gun corvettes were built by the Navy Board for the second
> experimental squadron." These were the Acorn and Satellite, constructed
> by me, and they proved the best vessels in the squadron, yet their
> excellent sailing properties are in no way noticed.
> In conclusion I beg to remark that it appears to me to be no way
> honourable for an author to attack a public body, or by name an
> individual holding an official situation, while he conceals himself for
> shelter beneath the ashes of the dead.

That last remark calls for an explanation. At the start of his own letter Sir Robert had mentioned that 'there was a general feeling amongst naval officers that the pamphlet was the posthumously published work of Vice Admiral Sir Charles Penrose', which gave weight to its assertions because of the character of that able, discerning, charming and very gracious man.[66] However, Seppings had written to Captain (later Vice Admiral) Sir John Coode, Penrose's son-in-law, who unequivocally disclaimed on his own part and on that of Lady Penrose and her family, any knowledge of the pamphlet. (It seems to the present author that a much more likely candidate for that authorship was Rear Admiral Samuel Brooking, of whom more later in this chapter.)

The excellent sailing qualities of HMS *Acorn* which 'were in no way noticed' by the anonymous author of the report which Sir Robert found so offensive, were however commented favourably upon by one of that vessel's lieutenants, Robert John Barrett. According to him, 'in light winds or moderate breezes, either sailing by the wind or going large, the *Acorn*'s superiority to any of the squadron was not manifest'. But, he went on, 'in strong breezes with a heavy sea, I never witnessed a flush vessel stand so stiff under her canvas, without straining either her rigging or her spars… in this weather, the *Acorn* was the only vessel in the squadron that succeeded in carrying both her fore and main-topgallant sails over double-reefed topsails and courses, without straining a yarn'.[67] Lieutenant Barrett can be rated a highly competent authority as before passing for lieutenant he had served as Master of several naval vessels and all masters were expert ship-handlers in their own right.

Fall-out from all that criticism was to haunt Robert Seppings for the rest of his career, and well into his retirement as we shall see. To add to those woes around this time, Ann, the wife of his dead brother John Milligen Seppings, together with the five boys of the eleven children she had borne him, were causing him trouble and concern. In a letter he wrote to his sister Helen dated 1 January 1827,[68] after praising the Laws nephews calling them 'respectable young men', he went on:

> I wish I could say as much for my poor brother's. His eldest son lived with me many months free of expense until his salary came due, and had withal some pounds of me, he was placed in a most respectable situation his income annually would have been by end of this year nearly £200 from which he could have keeped [sic] his distressed family but alas! his conduct has been such that they discharged him from the situation! he over head and heels in debt, and I understand that he is about to depart for Devon to add to the difficulties of his distressed family, without the hope of earning a shilling! Of course he never comes under my roof

---

[66] See article *Sir Charles Vinicombe Penrose* by *Nauticus*, Mariner's Mirror, Vol 29, 1943.
[67] See *U.S.J.* 1830, page 355.
[68] Packard Papers.

again: had he conducted himself correctly he might have rose to a salary of £700 per annum, but he is innate bad. The second [son] is a sailor, he has caused me much trouble, I am out of pocket by him last year £50 of which I never shall have a farthing. The third is a clerk in the Navy Office and has been with me more than twelve months free of expense. The fourth is now with me, he belongs to the College at Addiscombe a great thing it is, he will be sent out to the East Indies as an officer it was presented to me, by a Gentleman in consequence of certain drawings I arranged for the East India Company. After this youth is educated it will cost us at least £200 to fit him out, where is this to come from? Mrs. Seppings family that has been upon my poor brother will not give a sixpence! In fact they say so openly. It was a singular thing my poor unthinking brother should have married into such a stock. She is a poor silly woman, full of vanity without a shade of pretensions. I have long seen, what has come to pass, but I did not think her relatives so *bad.* Happy would it have been if it had pleased God to have taken my brother before he had made such a connection and then my latter days and that of my wife's and children would have been of a different description. There is another boy at home: I could provide for him but these people will not advance a sixpence to assist me! Silly woman, she was calling her children all sorts of names, without thinking the name they must bear in the world, without the fear of God before their eyes. There are five girls, four children. [In fact there were six girls with five of them at that time under the age of 13.] Ann [the eldest aged 20] will be married in midsummer. I have written you a longer letter than perhaps I shall ever again, for I have so much writing that I am tired. My wife and self have dreadful colds, and I grieve to say our dear Mary [Sir Robert's second eldest daughter] is in a very delicate state of health.

I find Mr. Dockerill is better, he is I believe a good man.[69]

Adieu. R. Seppings.

He added this postscript. "After what I have written in this hasty epistle you may suppose I have given up correspondence with Mrs. Seppings, that is not the case: she now finds out we are her only friends: and God knows a dear acquaintance she is, what should we all have been had my wife have been like her?"

---

[69] Joseph Dockerill a London tea merchant, was Sir Robert's nephew-in-law having married in 1815 Susan Elizabeth Pleasance, one of his sister Helen's two daughters.

To have wished his brother an earlier death in that way, supports a remark made by Brigadier Packard, to the effect that the career of Lt. John Milligen Seppings had been held back by a wife and recalcitrant children.[70] That Mrs. Ann Seppings was inclined to lack in some of the social niceties is also supported by a passage in a letter her husband John wrote to his sister Helen from Greenwich in May 1819.[71] 'How am I to begin to thank you for your very bountiful present so long since received… there is an apology from my wife due to you for not answering some former letter… I trust you will forgive us.' It seems that a gift, perhaps in the form of money, had been sent whilst John was away at sea and had not been acknowledged.

After Lt. John Milligen Seppings R.N. married Ann Marshal Lockyer in Plymouth on 1 April 1804, his wife took up residence in Lime Kiln Lane now called South Street, in Greenwich, and the first nine of their eleven children, including all five boys mentioned in Sir Robert's letter, were born there and christened in nearby St. Alfege (now Alphege) Church – the last two girls were born in Devon.

In age order the boys mentioned in that letter, were:

John Milligen Seppings, born 2 April 1805. It appears that sometime after leaving the position Sir Robert had arranged for him, he travelled out to India to work. He died at Mysore on 13 December 1879. Despite what Sir Robert thought of him, he seems to have made a success of his time in India.

Edmund Henry Seppings, born 6 December 1807. He joined the Royal Navy, probably with the help of Sir Robert, and rose to the rank of lieutenant. He was serving in that rank in HMS *Shannon* on 18 December 1829 when, at Bermuda, he was discharged into HMS *Ranger*. That ship's Muster Book under the heading 'Discharge Details' on 6 November 1830 when at Barbados, shows the word 'Run' against his name, the official naval term for 'deserted'. (See file ADM37/8340, National Archives.) Under the Naval Articles of War the maximum (and usual) sentence for that crime was death by hanging. However, Australian records show that he died at Grong Grong, in the remote Riverina District of New South Wales in May 1858, having earlier married there and fathered a family.

---

[70] Packard Papers.
[71] ibid.

Nicholas Lockyer Seppings, born 13 June 1810. He married Harriet Blogg at St. Pancras, London, 5 January 1836. It seems he made a success of his career for at the time of the 1851 Census, he described himself as a 'Gentleman in the Civil Service'; he was then living in Clerkenwell. He died at Wandsworth in May 1887.

Alworth Merriwether Seppings, born 26 July 1811. Educated as arranged by Sir Robert, at Addiscombe, Surrey, the school run by the HEIC for its civil service and military cadets. (This education was probably the form of recompense Sir Robert received for designing two of HEIC's ships as mentioned in Chapter 5.) In India he began his career as an Ensign in the HEIC Regiment of Artillery; on 2 June 1828 Alworth was promoted to 2nd. Lieutenant and later to full Lieutenant. On 19 August 1840 when still in that rank 'he was permitted to resign' from HEIC service. During his military career he had been reprimanded on at least two occasions. He died at Kensington in 1860.

William Lawless Seppings, born 31 December 1812. He too attended Addiscombe School at the expense of Sir Robert, and became a Lieutenant in the HEIC Army in India. On 22 February 1834 he married a 20-year old widow Isabella Georgiana Catherine White née Lane, at Bangalore. He appears to have died at Greenwich in 1845. His wife died at Bangalore on 31 October 1860.

(For details of the six daughters of the marriage between Lt. John Milligen Seppings and Ann Lockyer, see Appendix 1.)

Despite his protestations, Sir Robert had not given up corresponding with Ann Seppings and had helped her last son (as shown in the box above). Direct evidence of this appears in a letter he wrote in the following year to one of Ann's brothers, Edmund Lockyer, of George Street, Plymouth. (Sir Robert and Lockyer were joint executors of Lt. John Seppings' estate, including his residence at Culver House, Chudleigh.) It is also clear that although he was still helping the sons, he was also still angry with at least one of them and was extremely irritated with the name of another.

Navy Office, 7th November 1828.
My dear Sir,
I suppose that Mrs. Seppings has informed you that I have been fortunate as to procure a cadet's appointment for her younger son and that I have promised £60 to assist in fitting him out. This sum with others that I

have advanced for these youths is by no means convenient to me, or just to my children and grand children, which are many and I am anything but a rich man.

Mrs. Seppings states to me that she will send me £100. These sums – with some little additions, I hope will fit this youth out and pay his voyage. Nothing is then left but correct conduct in her son, and all will be well. These boys have been fortunate beyond all precedent, but they have been brought up to think the world was made for them. That youth Alworth gave me great trouble, and bills have come in which he contracted for articles such as fruit etc. The youth that is now about is I believe christened WILLIAM LAWLESS SEPPINGS. Now, really this name is very disorderly (it may sound well in Ireland, but does nor sound well in my ears). Could it not in this youth's commission be sunk? Mention this to the mother & favour me with your opinion touching this point.

I hope and trust, dear Sir, that you have arranged the money that was paid for the Chudleigh estate in the way we agreed upon.

I am sure you have plenty on your hands, but do set apart a little of your time at any easy period to settle this business, as well also that the Trust which you and myself are held responsible for is so clearly settled that neither of the executors will be called to an account; for it would be hard upon my children to part with the little that I may leave them. I told my better half and daughter that I was about to write to you and they requested that they might offer their best wishes to you,

> And believe me to be dear Sir,
> Faithfully yours.
> Robert. Seppings[72]

On top of all those troubles in his extended family we have already noted that in 1827 the health of his daughter Mary was causing him much concern. In consequence she together with Lady Seppings and the younger children, spent about five months of that year in the more salubrious air of Folkestone on the coast.

In that same year Sir Robert had to deal with another controversial and litigious travail. In a letter to his nephew Robert Gill in 1827, he wrote:

> From little time since an infamous libel was written against my professional character wherein it was stated that I had constructed a

---

[72] Transcript made by Christine Colthurst of a letter in the possession of Elsie Joyce Speirs nee Cosens (a direct descendant of Sir Robert).

ship that was lost at sea arising from her faulty building. The ship was a good ship but it so happened that I was *not* her Constructor. It was my desire to prosecute the Editor of the paper but my friends were against it and recommended an answer. This I complied with and the cap so fitted that the person has moved the Court of King's Bench that a criminal prosecution shall be commenced against me: this is not a very pleasant circumstance as it will cost me much trouble and expense.

It seems that the original alleged libel had been in a letter to the Editor of the *Maidstone Gazette* written by Captain Charles Phillips, a retired naval officer, who was now prosecuting Sir Robert for something he had written in his answer! Details are sparse because the case seems to have been settled out of court.

Then in the following year on 11 December the *London Globe* reported the following from the Bow Street Court.

A person called Williams was summoned before the sitting magistrate Sir Richard Bernie for having sent threatening letters to Sir Robert Seppings, one of the Commissioners of Woolwich Dockyard. The prisoner, with 370 other workers, was some time since discharged from the dockyard and shortly afterwards he memorialised for a pension, which after an investigation relative to his claim, was refused. He then commenced sending letters to Sir Robert Seppings one of which contained the passage:- 'I will teach you to know, Sir Robert, that a man, however in humble circumstances, will not be treated by you with impunity'. Bernie [to the prisoner], "You acknowledge yourself to be the writer of this letter?" Prisoner, "I do, Sir Richard." "And of this, which states that you would sooner be confined in prison than remain as you are?" Prisoner, "Yes Sir." Bernie, "I have little doubt that but you have committed an offence which subject you to greater punishment than imprisonment." The Secretary of the Commissioners stated that although Sir Robert Seppings had been so annoyed, he only wished the prisoner could be prevented from doing so in future. Sir Richard Bernie represented to the Prisoner the nature of his offence, and discharged him after an admonition to write no more threatening letters.

It seems there was no way that controversy was ever going to leave Robert Seppings alone. In 1816 Rear Admiral Samuel Brooking (c.1754-1834), who after his retirement from the navy for health reasons in about 1800 had become one of the most prolific correspondents on naval affairs in the

United Services Journal, had written directly to Sir Robert proposing a plan to reduce the size of the rudder by tapering it towards the back, and thereby significantly reducing its overall weight. The principle was condemned in the following words in a letter signed by Seppings: 'The surveyors cannot recommend its adoption as the rudder must be put over many degrees more than is at present necessary, before the same effect would be produced.'

Then in 1822 Brooking took this matter up again in an open letter to Sir Robert published in the *United Services Journal.* This time his view was backed by a panel of seven senior naval officers stating that they, 'all were agreed in that respect, that reducing the rudder by tapering towards the after end would be advantageous'. Brooking kept this up in the Journal and eventually Sir Robert replied in kind, saying that the admiral had, 'bent his thoughts on a trifle, and worked himself up to believe it was a matter of importance'. (As an aside it is of interest to note that the pages of the *Journal* record several instances of people laying claim to the plans Brooking professed as being his own.)

Sir Robert's reply caused the admiral to write another open letter dated 24 November 1831.[73] Reiterating what has been outlined above, he then wrote:
"I forbear Sir Robert, making any further comment than by stating (with all due respect to your scientific judgement and highly responsible station), that had experienced seamen, instead of surveyors,been my judges in 1816 and in 1822, not one ship belonging to His Majesty would years ago have been without a reduced tapered rudder, working in a grooved stern-post; and I must look to you now, as an act of justice to myself, and as a duty to the service, to second me in my intended application to be allowed to try my plans, of the rudder and sail, on some vessel on the home station. Much, much as may be said on the subject, I conclude,
Sir Robert,
Your obedient servant,
Samuel Brooking
[Note: A tapered rudder was brought in later, but not during Sir Robert's short time left as Surveyor.]

Rear Admiral Samuel Brooking seems a likely candidate for the authorship of that anonymously published pamphlet by 'Flag Officer' mentioned earlier

---

[73] *U.S.J.* 1832.

in this chapter. According to his obituary in *Gentleman's Magazine* of 1834, after Brooking retired 'his mind was continuously with the service, and he was numbered as one of the correspondents of the *United Services Journal*'. Not much effort, one supposes, is required to change a keen letter writer into a pamphleteer, especially if the pamphlet was largely directed at a man the pamphleteer had previously found cause to criticize.

The last major ships built from plans drawn by Seppings were three 98-gun two-deckers of the *Rodney* class. Although their keels were laid in 1827, all three were launched well after he left the service in 1832. They were HMS *Rodney*, launched at Pembroke Dockyard in 1833; HMS *Nile* launched at Plymouth in 1839; and HMS *London* launched at Chatham in 1840. In the 1850s all three were fitted with screw propulsion and 500 horse-power engines. In 1876 the *Nile* was renamed *Conway* and became famous as a training ship for Merchant Navy officers until 1953 when she was wrecked in the Menai Straits.[74]

Amongst the last of the smaller sailing ships designed by him were the naval packet *Seagull* 1831, the schooner-tenders *Hornet* 1831 and *Spider* 1835, and the sloops *Griffin* and *Forester* in 1832. All these vessels were built from imported cedar, which indicates his constant interest in using different kinds of timber.

---

[74] In latter years the *Conway*'s alumni included the poet laureate John Masefield and the politician Ian Duncan Smith.

8
The Last Years in Office

When the new Whig government of Earl Grey took office in 1830, Sir James Graham was appointed First Lord of the Admiralty. He immediately set about the task of reducing the Naval Estimates and in the process came under severe criticism in the House of Commons. One of his fiercest critics was the Tory MP for Plymouth who was also Comptroller of the Navy Board, Admiral Sir Thomas Byam Martin. That situation could not last of course, and Byam Martin was dismissed from his post on 2 November 1831. In June of the following year the post of Comptroller was abolished altogether and the duties of the Navy Board were amalgamated with those of the Board of Admiralty. So now, Sir Robert Seppings, Surveyor of the Navy, who may well have been a Tory like his friend Byam Martin, was directly responsible to the First Lord, who was a Whig. Furthermore, in the months leading up to the amalgamation of the two Boards there had been talk that the post of Surveyor was also to be abolished and replaced by some other title with altered duties attached to the holder of it. That particular change did not take place in fact until 1861; nevertheless it was all very unsettling, and Seppings must have realized that the writing was on the wall and that his days in office were numbered. The end indeed came in 1832.

On the home front his second daughter Mary married naval surgeon Robert Armstrong M.D. on 24 April 1832 at the Church of St. Mary le Strand.[75] (For more family information see Appendix I.) This turned out to be the very last family function organised by Sir Robert from his official residence in Somerset Place. It was probably around this time that a contemporary wrote that the Seppings daughters were noted for their 'beauty, height and bearing'. A few years later, the Reverend Sydney Smith, Canon of St. Paul's Cathedral and a noted contributor to the *Edinburgh Review*, wrote of 'the swan-necked Miss Seppings'. (Two portraits of Louisa Seppings are known to exist, one before her marriage and a later one. The image reproduced in this book confirms that she was rather beautiful and had a long slender neck.[76])

Edward Milligen Beloe, the author of the entry about Sir Robert Seppings in the first edition of the *Dictionary of National Biography*, wrote that, 'When in 1832 Sir James Graham… began a reform of naval administration,

---

[75] *Sherbourne Mercury* 14 May 1832.
[76] This portrait was the property of Mrs.Joyce Speirs (nee Cozens) a direct descendant of Louisa, until it was sold in auction at Aldridge of Bath on 5 September 2000.

Seppings resigned on 12 June 1832'. In fact it was not at all like that. (Beloe was distantly related to Sir Robert, one of whose nieces had married a William Beloe.)

According to *Hansard*, the official record of all that goes on in the House of Commons, a few months after Seppings left office, Byam Martin stood up and spoke thus:

> 'I understand that the [post of] Surveyor of the Navy is to be continued, so why was Sir Robert Seppings dismissed? Never in the course of my life have I met with so diligent, so faithful, so honest, a public servant. He was a most respectable man who laboured in the public service for fifty years without thinking of his own concerns, and yet he was dismissed.'

So the admiral knew his friend had been dismissed. To hurrahs he then added,

> 'That requires explanation. His mode of putting ships together was most useful and its excellence proved by every nation having adopted it. I know that some people had most unworthily tried to raise prejudices against Sir Robert Seppings, but his name will be remembered with honour when those of his traducers would have sunk into contempt and oblivion. As long as ships float on the ocean, Sir Robert Seppings will be respected.'

Let us hear what Seppings himself wrote concerning his leaving of office; it appeared in an article he wrote in the *United Service Journal*, dated 2 January 1834 which was published under the heading *Sir Robert Seppings, in Explanation of his Official Conduct*.[77] He wrote that his character had lately been attacked with 'most gross misrepresentations' in various newspapers and in one magazine article in particular (of which more in the next chapter) and that whilst, 'contempt is, in general, the most effectual means of silencing the voice of slander', because of the reiterated attacks, 'silence on my part might…be construed into an admission that the charges were well founded'. Some of these attacks accused him of undermining the work of the man who succeeded him in the post of Surveyor, Captain William Symonds, and not only that, of attempting to undermine the authority of the First Lord of the Admiralty Sir John Graham. Seppings went on, 'When my removal from office was contemplated, it is well known that no interest was employed by me, nor by any friend of mine at my request, to be allowed to continue in office; and, although attached to pursuits which had been the study of my whole life, a feeling of delicacy would have prevented me from even entering a dockyard without first obtaining permission from Sir J. Graham'.

---

[77] *United Services Journal*, 1834, Part 1.

Because Seppings himself wrote of having been removed from office and his friend Byam Martin had said 'he was dismissed', plus the fact that the editors of several newspapers had also written that he was 'pushed from office', the notion that he resigned voluntarily must be discarded. It may be that in the end he proffered his resignation but if that was so, it is clear that he was pressured into doing so.

He was then 65 years of age. He had always, to paraphrase Byam Martin's words, worked long and laborious hours, sacrificed his leisure time, and on more than a few occasions had had to fight off the jealousy and prejudice of others. On top of that he had contended with powerful traditionalists over such matters as the introduction of new shipbuilding methods and the introduction of new sorts of wood, and of iron fittings. All that must have affected his health. So once the initial shock of his removal had lessened, maybe he experienced some measure of relief.

It turned out that he was the very last Surveyor of the Navy to have started out as a dockyard apprentice and worked his way up to the post, for within twenty-four hours of his leaving, Captain William Symonds, a naval officer, was appointed in his place and the Admiralty never again returned to the old practice.

Before we deal with Sir Robert's retirement years, it will be useful to give a short account of Captain Symonds period in office and what eventually happened to the post of Surveyor. Symonds did not enjoy a quiescent tenure. Throughout it, acrimonious debates went on similar to those that had characterized his predecessor's last years in office. In a letter to Seppings, Sir James Graham once wrote, 'Except on matters of religion, I do not know of any difference of opinion which has been attended with so much bitterness – so much anger – so much resentment, as the merits of Sir W. Symonds and the virtues of his ships'. (That indicates that Graham must still have been on reasonably good terms with Seppings and kept in touch with him at least four years into his retirement, because Captain Symonds did not receive his knighthood until 1836.)

Symonds was accused of 'meddling in design', and whilst his ships were sometimes faster and were definitely more stable than other comparable ships, they were subject to excessive rolling thus putting great stress on hulls, masts and rigging; indeed, the heavy lurch over to the lee side to which they were prone became almost proverbial. At various trials made in 1835 and

1836, his supporters made claim to the success of the vessels designed by him, the 50-gun frigate HMS *Vernon* launched in 1832 at Woolwich being a case in point. However, Parliamentary Papers of 6 May 1836, contain a summary of a total of 24 trials held between that ship and the 50-gun *Barham* in the Mediterranean in November and December 1835.[78] The papers contained a report signed by Captain Sir William Elliott, and countersigned by Mr. Bellamy, master, on those trials, and based on that report the Papers concluded: 'So far from bearing out the assertion that the *Vernon* was always superior, this proves on the contrary, that when in competition with a ship of similar class and equal warlike capabilities, she was beaten upon all points of sailing at least four times as often as she beat her adversary.' Furthermore, when HMS *Pique*, designed by Symonds, held 8 trials with the Seppings' designed HMS *Castor*, the latter 'won' five times.

All this criticism eventually caused the Admiralty to change the terms of Symonds' job description, to use a modern phrase. Ship design was no longer to be a major part of the Surveyor's task; instead he was to be assisted in that by a committee. He found himself unable to agree with this and so resigned in 1847. (He left with a pension of £500 a year, which may provide an indication of the size of the one Seppings had enjoyed from 1832.)

Symonds' successor as Surveyor was another naval officer, Captain (later Admiral) Sir Baldwin Wake Walker, Baronet. His remit forbad him to design ships without the aid of two former students of the long defunct School of Naval Architecture, one of whom was called Isaac Watts. In 1858 Walker produced the specifications (reportedly with some reluctance because he still preferred wooden-hulled ships) for the navy's first iron-clad, HMS *Warrior* which Watts went on to design. He retired in 1861 and died at Diss in Norfolk in 1876. His place, but under the new title Chief Constructor of the Navy (one still in use today), was taken by Isaac Watts (1797-1876), which proves that the Rev. Inman's old School of Naval Architecture did leave a legacy.

At South Kensington, London, the Royal School of Naval Architecture and Marine Engineering was founded in 1864. Although this was not to be the final change in this important branch of the navy, it can be said that under that resounding title the training of shipbuilding apprentices in the navy had come of age.

---

[78] The *Barham* was launched as a 74-gun 3rd Rate at a private firm on the Thames at Blackwall in 1811. In 1826 she was 'cut down' and reduced to a 50-gun frigate at Woolwich Dockyard.

9

Unquiet Retirement in Somerset: the Acrimonious Correspondence with Captain Frederick Marryat

It was reported in the Irish newspaper *Cork Constitution* of 28 July 1832, that 'Sir Robert and Lady Seppings took passage from London in the *Confiance* for Bridport'. (This was almost certainly the paddle-steamer HMS *Confiance*, built at Woolwich five years earlier to Sir Robert's design.) As Bridport in West Dorset is less than thirty miles from Taunton in Somerset where the couple were to set up home, perhaps they made that summer sea voyage because Lady Charlotte's health was not up to the arduous coach journey from London, or maybe they preferred to travel in a ship capable of carrying the family together with their belongings.

They had taken out a lease on a large house at Taunton called *Vivary* at No.3 Mount Terrace situated in one of the most fashionable parts of the town and which overlooked parkland. *Vivary* was but a short carriage ride from St. Mary Magdalene Church at which they were to become regular worshippers. In a letter dated 27 June 1832 to her cousin Robert Gill, Helen Seppings, Sir Robert's youngest daughter wrote that the house was "about five minutes from town, the rent including taxes and everything is £150 per annum, which certainly is high for the country, though I ought to have told you for the above sum three acres of meadow land, coach house and stables, are included".[79] Perhaps Taunton was chosen as the place for their retirement because Seppings' old friend Joseph Whidbey had been domiciled there since 1830; he lived in St. James House, not too far way from *Vivary* and even closer to the town centre.

Vivary was large enough to cope with becoming a temporary base for the couple's eldest son, John Milligen Seppings and his family when they returned to England on leave from India in early 1833. Sir Robert was back in London on business and residing at 34 Bridge Street, Blackfriars, when on 19 April of that year he wrote this in a letter to his nephew Robert Gill in Manchester.

---

[79] Packard Papers.

'Have been in this great city since last Monday week and … it is uncertain
when I shall leave … hope to have it in my power to pay you a visit the
end of this month or the beginning of next, and John [his son] who at
this time is at Taunton and ere long will I believe proceed to Pembroke
and see his brother [the invalid Andrew], and from thence to you.'
(This is yet another confirmation of how close knit was the Seppings family.)

If the presence of Joseph Whidbey at Taunton had indeed been the reason
for Seppings' decision to reside there, then it appears that matters may not
have worked out quite as intended. Apart from the fact that in a little more
than a year Whidbey was dead (he was buried on 9 October 1833 in St. James
Churchyard where his tombstone can still be seen), it seems there had been
some kind of falling out between the two. In his will of 1832, Whidbey, a
bachelor, had appointed Seppings and a man called Woodford as joint
trustees, with Seppings as the residuary legatee. In May 1833, however,
Whidbey made another will which substituted a certain Mr. Fowler, a builder,
as trustee in place of Sir Robert, who now received a specific legacy of £100.
During an Assize Court case held in August 1834 in which he was the plaintiff,
Woodford was reported as having told one of the witnesses that Whidbey
had said that he had 'had a difference with Sir Robert Seppings'. The details
of the case as reported in the *Taunton Courier* and other newspapers are sparse
and unclear, but it seems that Sir Robert and Captain (later Admiral) Richard
Arthur together with several other naval officers, 'conceived the deceased to be
incompetent to make a new will', but as they 'did not concur in their evidence'
the jury returned a verdict for the plaintiff. The *Taunton Courier* later reported
under the heading 'Taunton and Somerset Hospital', that, 'Mr. Whidbey
bequeathed a legacy of £100 to Sir Robert Seppings who by deed of gift
made over the same less duty and costs to the trustees of that hospital'.

Because Taunton is situated not too far away from the main coaching route
between London, where the Navy Board was situated, and the port of
Plymouth, one can be fairly certain that Sir Robert was frequently visited
by naval officers when they travelled between those two places. Some of
those officers would have been serving in ships built to his designs, so who
better to turn to for information and advice on such matters as ballasting
and stability? Perhaps some came only for a yarn, or to exchange family
news for one must not forget that through the marriage of his wife's sister
Martha, he was connected to the extensive Dacres dynasty of naval officers.

In 1833 Sir Robert commissioned William Bradley to paint his portrait in oils. Bradley (1801-1857) enjoyed a large patronage and was known for producing 'striking and intellectual likeness's'. This portrait is now in the keeping of the National Maritime Museum at Greenwich and is the one used as an illustration in the *Dictionary of National Biography*. It is possible that a portrait of Lady Charlotte was also commissioned at this time, for an image of her alongside a copy of the one of her husband, is now on display in the Church of St. Mary Magdalene, Taunton. Seppings may have got the idea of using Bradley from his nephew Robert Gill, for the artist had painted a portrait of Gill in 1831.[80]

The portrait of Sir Robert depicted in this work has never previously been published. It is by the painter John Prescott Knight (1803-1881). It depicts the sitter full-face and holding a pair of brass dividers. According to H. Dyson, onetime Curator of the Stafford Library, Museum and Art Gallery, who catalogued Knight's pictures, this was one of the artist's early portraits and was exhibited at the Royal Academy exhibition of 1835, so is a slightly later image than the one at Greenwich.[81]

Professional controversy continued to dog Sir Robert into his retirement. In 1833 his adversary was none other than one of the most successful novelists of the age, Captain Frederick Marryat R.N. who wrote his books under the name 'Captain Marryat'.[82]

Marryat (1792-1848) had once served as midshipman in a frigate under the command of the dashing Lord Cochrane whose exploits later served as inspiration for some of his novels (not to mention those of several 20th century authors of naval fiction). So popular were his sea novels, it is possible that through them he became the best recruiting agent the navy ever had.

---

[80] The oil on canvas portrait of Robert Gill is reported to have been painted when he was about 35. It was gifted to the Elmbridge Museum in Esher, Surrey, from the estate of Mrs. Madeline Allen née Gill in 1986. Elmbridge also holds two double portraits in pastel of Frederica and Madeline, and Mary and Eleanor, Robert Gill's four daughters. These portraits by Charles Alan Duval, are dated 1858. Duval (1810-1872) was noted for his pastels.

[81] Letters from H. Dyson in 1964 to Miss Dora Mary Puttock, great granddaughter of Lt. John Milligen Seppings R.N., and her nephew Christopher John Seppings Colthurst.

[82] None of the several biographies of Marryat, including his daughter's account called *Life and Letters*, make any mention of the Seppings/Marryat controversy although it was common knowledge at the time.

He had a distinguished naval career that covered every sea from the eastern coast of America to the coast of Burma in the East. He invented a type of lifeboat, and more importantly, a widely used code of signals called after him that became the basis of the first International Code of Signals. He resigned his commission in 1830 to take up writing full-time. He was an acquaintance of Charles Dickens. Some of his novels were first serialised in *The Metropolitan Magazine* of which he was to be part owner and editor between 1832-1835. From early in life he suffered from haemoptysis of which the principal symptom is the spitting-up of blood from the lungs. Maybe it was that, plus the early deaths of three of his four sons, that caused him to become volatile and unstable, and sometimes downright abusive in some of his published articles and letters. He purchased 1,000 acres of farmland at Langham in Norfolk in 1830 that were worked by two tenant farmers. Towards the end of his life he lived in the Manor Cottage in that village and died there in 1848.[83]

Early in 1833, the year following the dismissal of Sir Robert Seppings and the appointment of Captain Symonds in his place, a pamphlet was published called *An Apology for English Ship Builders*. Written anonymously it received a wide circulation. It's main thrust was to show that it had been unnecessary and wrong for the country to look to the cadre of naval officers for its Naval Architects when it had many able shipwrights including graduates of the School of Naval Architecture who could do the job better. It could be described therefore as being pro-Sir Robert and anti-Symonds, his successor.

In the November 1833 issue of *The Metropolitan Magazine* Marryat took up his pen in support of his friend Symonds, and used it like a sword.[84] Flaying into that *Apology*, he began:
'This is a plausible and well written pamphlet, assuming a mask of humility to obtain its ends, and a deferential respect to the First Lord of the Admiralty which is completely at variance with the whole tenor of its argument and assertions. It has evidently been submitted to the scrutiny of many, has been carefully revised and corrected, and the sentences weighed previous to publication. We think we can put our finger upon several passages and ascribe them to their true writers.

---

[83] Captain Marryat is buried in a large tomb in the churchyard of St. Andrew & St. Mary, Langham. There are notices inside the church concerning his career and achievements.

[84] *The Metropolitan Magazine*, Vol.8, November 1833. Marryat's article, which ran to seven pages, was entitled *School of Naval Architecture*, and was signed 'F.M.' as were several other of his articles during this period.

We can trace suggestions from the ex Navy Board, ex Surveyor, and School of Naval Architecture, separately and conjointly in this little work, which we consider it our duty to refute, because it is well, apparently temperately written, and has we know, produced a greater sensation than these brochures usually do.'

After that Marryat added extra sharpness to his pen. After praising Symonds and his work in several ways, he cut loose. He named Sir Robert Sepping and called him a 'dockyard matey', a naval officer's insult reserved for someone low in estimation, and said he was 'everything but a sensible man or a gentleman'. Marryat's physical affliction must really have been playing him up, for there was more, much more of the same ilk. He said, 'the errors of Sir Robert Seppings are becoming every day more apparent', and then went on, 'During the whole period of his holding the situation, he did not build a good ship – the only one approximating to merit was the Castor whose lines after she was laid down were altered so as to steal upon the models of Captain Symonds'. [Marryat was here referring to Symond's plans for the *Vernon*.] He went on to name several other ships that had been rebuilt and altered during Seppings' regime and accused him of having 'spoilt' them.

Following that diatribe Marryat had the audacity to write:
'But it is not our object in this paper to enter upon the demerits of Sir Robert Seppings; we should leave him for the present with the remark that Sir James Graham acted most judiciously in removing him from his situation.'

Marryat also took swipes at Byam Martin the 'ex Navy Board' of his introduction. But perhaps he saved his worst vituperation for the ex-students of the School of Naval Architecture who were the least able amongst his targets to answer back. He listed many by name and made particularly snide and totally uncalled for remarks about their origins

Sir Robert Seppings could and did answer back, 'in a reply full of dignity, that so completely exposed Captain Marryat's pretensions, that we really believe he has been quite ashamed of the course he then took, ever since', wrote a commentator in 1847, the year before Marryat's death.[85]

---

[85] See *Review of the Course Pursued by the Shipbuilding Department of the Admiralty, 1832-1847*, published White Stevens, Plymouth 1847.

In Seppings' reply dated 2 January 1834, (which has already been quoted from in this book) and which was published in the *United Services Journal* under the heading *Sir Robt. Seppings, In Explanation Of His Official Conduct*, after giving his reasons for answering in this way, he went on:

'For some time I was at a loss to understand what offence I had given to Captain Marryat… to induce him so far to forget the respect which he owes to himself as an officer, as to animadvert on my character in language so coarse and scurrilous, and so repugnant to good taste and good feeling. Now, however he has… [written] the most calumnious and unfounded statements, he must take the consequences of his own indiscretion, and vindicate his character for veracity in the manner he may consider most eligible.'

After stating that Marryat had pretty broadly asserted that he had had some share in the writing and correcting of the *Apology* pamphlet, Seppings wrote:

'I can most unequivocally declare, that I never saw nor heard of the pamphlet… until at some time after its publication; that I had no knowledge of the author; nor held any communications with him, either prior to or since its publication.'

Later on:

'When the reviewer asserts that I have "never built a good ship", he probably expresses his individual opinion: he may even publish his opinion if he thinks proper, and endeavour to convince his readers… It is in matters of fact that I have to do on the present occasion. With reference to the Castor, "whose lines (it is alleged) were altered so as to steal upon the models of Captain Symonds", I can only reply that no alteration was made in the lines of that ship, and that it was impossible any such theft as he alludes to could have been committed, as the frame of the Castor was in progress, and far advanced towards completion, before the building of the Vernon was sanctioned by the Admiralty. The forms of the two ships are totally different.'

In his article Marryat had also boasted of the 'intuitive knowledge' that seamen develop over the years about the comparative merits of different ships. There is no doubt that that faculty does exist, for experience obviously teaches, but Marryat had tended to overplay it by designating Symond's methods as the 'Intituitive School of Shipbuilding'. Seppings threw this back in Marryat's face, when he wrote:

'That boasted "intuitive knowledge", however, has already with him proved fallacious; and it might have been presumed, that the melancholy catastrophe which resulted from his self-willed and reckless indifference to the opinion of practical men would have made a lasting impression on his memory, and disposed him in future to entertain some doubts of his own fallibility. The circumstance to which I allude he well remembers, and perfectly understands the application.'

In an otherwise staid and dignified answer which showed that just about everything Marryat had written in his scurrilous article had no basis in truth, this was the nearest Sir Robert got to being nasty himself.

The 'melancholy catastrophe' he referred to needs an explanation. That event had taken place four years earlier during Marryat's very last command, that of the frigate HMS *Ariadne* between 1828 and 1830. His mission in that command had been partly hydrographic, namely to search for shoals and unmarked reefs around the Portuguese-owned Azores Islands and Madeira, but, much more importantly, it was a semi-diplomatic one. Portugal was then in the throes of revolution and the British Government was concerned over the future of those strategically placed Atlantic islands and so the *Ariadne* was there to show the flag. Late in 1829 the *Ariadne* called in at San Miguel, the most southerly of the Azores, to find that an American 180-ton schooner, the *Samuel Smith*, had been run ashore in a sandy cove after striking a reef and damaging her hull. Her owner/master had decided, because there were no carpenters on the island capable of repairing her, to put the vessel and her stores up for auction. Marryat was struck by the beauty of her lines – she was in fact well-known as a fast sailer – and aware, in the words of his subsequent report to the Admiralty, 'that the Navy Board were purchasing vessels of this description for Tenders, and thinking that even as a model she was valuable, I repaired to the Schooner, taking with me the 1st Lieutenant, Carpenter and Carpenter's Mate, before I would decide upon the purchase'. The result was that he, disregarding the pessimism of some of his officers, decided to buy her. He paid £260 for her out of his own funds. Then, by working day and night, the ship was repaired by the *Ariadne* carpenters and successfully refloated and gotten over the reef that had caused the damage in the first place. It was a brilliant piece of seamanship as would be expected of a captain of Marryat's experience and calibre. He placed Master's Mate Philip Salmon on board to command the purchased craft with ten volunteers from his crew, but on the way to Madeira the two ships parted company and the schooner was never heard of again and so was presumed lost with all hands.[86] After *Ariadne* arrived back home in 1830 the Navy Board set up a Court of Enquiry at which Marryat and all his officers were questioned about the event, and it brought in the following verdict. 'Their Lordships consider that Captain Marryat was not justified in purchasing the vessel in question and placing in her men of the *Ariadne*, not having been desired or authorised to do so by either the Navy Board or the Admiralty.'[87] Not only that, a sum of £40, the estimated cost of the repairs carried out on the schooner by the *Ariadne*'s carpenters, was mulcted from his salary. Marryat was much aggrieved by all this, and that plus the success of his latest book, caused him to resign from the navy in that same year.

Because Marryat in his article had not only accused Sir Robert of never having designed a good ship, but had also asserted that he had spoilt others that he had had nothing at all to do with, towards the end of his reply, Sir Robert wrote this:

'For the information of those who may desire to know what ships have been constructed by me, and with a view of affording my detractors an opportunity of exerting their genius in writing reviews, I beg to annex a list of ships for whose qualities I consider myself responsible. With those built by others, I had no more concern than Captain Marryat or his associates.'

This is his list:

'Ships and vessels built and building, constructed by Sir Robert Seppings, viz:- London, Nile, Rodney, 98 guns each; Calcutta, 84; Castor, Amphion, 36 guns each; Andromache, Calliope, Conway, Imogene, Tyne, 28 guns each.

Sloops:- Pylades, Satellite, Scout, Pheasant, Redwing.

Schooners:- Cockatrice, Hornet, Seagull, Spider, Viper.

Cutters:- Sparrow, Jackdaw, Lark, Magpie, Quail, Raven, Starling.

Steam-Vessels:- About eleven in number.

[Author's note: if the uncommissioned Congo is included, there were twelve.] N.B. The seven frigates, viz., the Java, Portland, Chichester, Lancaster, Southampton, Winchester, and Worcester, mounting 52 guns each, and similar to each other, were not constructed by me; but after the Java was launched, I advised the bows of the others to be made fuller, which was directed to be done.'

In view of its source, that list can be considered definitive.

---

[86] ADM 1/2205/49, National Archives.
[87] ADM 1/2205/55.

10
The Final Years

Lady Charlotte Seppings who, according to letters from Sir Robert and his daughters to Robert Gill, had been in increasingly bad health for several years, did not long survive the move to Somerset. London's *Morning Post* for 26 November 1834 carried the following obituary. 'At the Vivary, Taunton, on the morning of the 23rd inst., died Charlotte the beloved wife of Sir Robert Seppings. She was of quiet unaffected piety, neatly bearing the fruits of the spirit of love'. The 29 November 1834 edition of the *Norwich Mercury* presents us with a little more information about her death and about her natal family. Lady Charlotte it recorded, 'died after a 3-day illness. She was the sister of Mrs. Robinson of this city'. Because Sir Robert and his wife had spent nearly all their lives in each other's company, one concludes he must have been devastated by her loss. She was buried in St. Mary Magdalene Church, Taunton. After her death Sir Robert was looked after by his daughter-in-law Marianne, whose husband John was away in Calcutta, and by her daughter Charlotte.

Five months after Lady Charlotte's death, Louisa the couple's second youngest daughter then aged twenty-four, married on 11 March 1835 Edward Lock in that same church. Lock, born in Oxford in 1785, was fifty and so over twice his wife's age. They had two children, Helen born in 1836, and Edward Seppings (yet another example of the use of Seppings as a Christian name) in 1838.

Edward Lock was the son of Sir Joseph Lock, a wealthy goldsmith and banker (University & City Bank), and twice Mayor of Oxford. Joseph Lock had rather remarkably been knighted by mistake, for the honour was meant to have been bestowed upon the city's long standing Town Clerk, one William Elias Taunton. In 1813 the Prince Regent who was in the city accompanied by some of the Allied Sovereigns (the Napoleonic Wars still had another two years to run), was there to do the honours. Evidently, there was a mix-up in the standard protocol for handling the preliminary address and the necessary documentation, and this caused the Prince to ask Mayor Lock, who was there as one of Taunton's supporters, to kneel and dubbed him knight! Once dubbed it seems you stayed dubbed no matter what, for although the error was soon pointed out, there was no way His Royal Highness was going to lose face in front of his illustrious guests, so everything stayed as it was. (Taunton did eventually receive his knighthood.)

At the time of the 1841 Census Edward Lock with his wife Louisa and their two children were living at Sir Joseph Lock's town house in Headington, Oxford. (Lock senior was then living at the stately home he had built for himself, Bury Knowle House.) Sir Joseph died in 1844, and divided his estate between Edward and his only other surviving child who by that time had become Mrs. Maria Ballachey. Edward soon left Oxford and by the time of the 1851 Census he and Louisa were living at Halcon Lodge, West Monckton, near Taunton. Edward Lock died aged 74 in 1859. In the following year his widow Louisa married the Rev. William du Sautoy at Abingdon.

When the childless Mrs. Ballachey died, she left her entire estate to her nephew, Edward Seppings Lock.

On or about 14 November 1835, Sir Robert paid a visit to Plymouth Dockyard to view HMS *Rodney* (built to one of his designs at Pembroke Dock and launched in 1833), which was now being fitted out for service. 'Sir Robert Seppings is here', proclaimed the local newspaper. 'He has visited the Yard and narrowly examined the *Rodney*; she certainly is a very splendid ship'. London's *Morning Advertiser* for 23 November provides us with more information about that visit. 'The worthy ex-surveyor has been here for two or three weeks past, looking into her [the ship's] fittings', which rather implied the visit was an official one. He was probably wined and dined at some time during that period by its commander, Captain Hyde Parker. (This Hyde Parker was the son of Admiral Sir Hyde Parker who had been in command of the fleet at the Battle of Copenhagen in 1801 at which Nelson so distinguished himself.)

In 1836 the University of Oxford conferred upon Sir Robert an honorary Doctorate in Civil Law. At around this same time he received many other honours from both home and abroad, including being made an Honorary Member of the Cambridge Philosophical Society. In July of that same year we find him, according to London's *Morning Post*, attending along with dozens of other celebrities, a Fete Chametre in the Royal Vauxhall Gardens in London. This was an outdoor festival and garden party, always held in 'picturesque and pastoral settings'.

On 7 March 1837 his youngest daughter Helen Milligen Seppings, then 25, married in St. Mary Magdalene, Taunton, one Daniel Godfrey, from Abingdon. One of the witnesses was Marianne, her sister-in-law.

On the very next day the *Taunton Courier & Western Advertiser* for 8 March carried the following item.

To Let.
Family Home to be let.
Sir Robert Seppings will vacate at or before midsummer,
The Vivary.
3 to 7 years.

That was followed by a full description of the property. It is not known whether Sir Robert did vacate the property and, if he did, where he took up alternative accommodation.

Anyway, when Sir Robert Seppings died of epilepsy on Saturday 25 April 1840, aged 72, he was still in Taunton. An obituary under the heading 'Death of Sir Robert Seppings' appeared in the *Taunton Courier* edition published a few days after his death and many others appeared in newspapers all over the land. For example the *Commercial Chronicle* of the city of Belfast, one day to grow into one of he world's major shipbuilding centres, published this in its edition dated 2 May. 'It is with sincere regret that we have to announce the death of the distinguished naval architect to whose science Old England stands indebted for so many of her wooden walls. We allude to Sir Robert Seppings, FRS, for so many years surveyor of the British navy. Sir Robert commenced his career as a naval architect under the late Sir John Henslow, and served his country faithfully in that capacity for nearly 50 years. His improvements in shipbuilding were numerous and important.'
He was buried in St. Mary Magdalene Church, in the chancel of which there is memorial tablet to the memory of him and his wife. It was erected by their son John Milligen Seppings. It is about three feet high and stands about 10 feet from the ground and over the Priest's door. The words on it read:-

Sacred to the Memory of Sir Robert Seppings F.R.S., Surveyor of the Royal Navy who died at Taunton 25th April 1840 aged 72 after serving his country fifty years.
"To his abilities and exertions this Country is mainly indebted for its most valuable improvements in Naval Architecture which will confer a lasting benefit on the British Nation" – from the Report of the

Committee of Finance of the House of Commons 30th April 1819.
Sacred to the memory of Charlotte the beloved wife of Sir Robert
Seppings late Chief Surveyor of His Majesty's Navy. She departed this
life the 23rd November 1834 aged 64 years.
                    Her life was guided by Truth.

This one-time messenger boy from Norfolk left behind a substantial
record of achievement that rivals and arguably surpasses, that of any of his
predecessors and successors in the post of Surveyor of the Navy. It is perhaps
ironic that he, one of the greatest naval architects of the era of wooden ships,
came along almost at the end of their day. During his years as Surveyor,
Robert Seppings had scrutinized and questioned many of the old ways of
constructing wooden ships and then gone on to either overhaul or change
more than a few of them; and he did that in the face of stiff and stubborn
opposition from powerful people connected with the Admiralty who did
not care much for change in any form. The innovations he introduced during
those last decades of the 'wooden-walls' navy were fundamental in enhancing
the power of British naval vessels, not only because stronger ships could
carry bigger guns, but also because they were better protected against enemy
return fire. Furthermore, they were copied all around the world. The
improvements and good practices initiated by him in looking after timber
before, during and after the construction of ships ensured they had a longer
working life. (In November 1835 his successor was able to report that there
was no dry rot in the fleet.) The draughts of many of the ships built during
his tenure in office bear his signature as designer, and provide testament to
his expertise in that field. His name can be found in every book or treatise
published in Britain or abroad on the subject of 19th century shipbuilding.
And it must never be forgotten that many of his early inventions and
innovations that so improved the performance of the Royal Navy, came into
effect at the time Britain was in the gravest peril with Napoleon poised to
attack across the Channel.

'Living' testimonies to his genius are to be found in the preserved *Trincomalee*
at Hartlepool, and even more so in the preserved frigate *Unicorn* at Dundee,
the latter roofed over almost exactly as she was when launched at Chatham
in 1824. He even left his mark in HMS *Victory* at Portsmouth; for during what
was called a 'middling refit' to that ship in 1814-16, her original beak-head
bow was replaced with a Seppings' built-up one. (Soon after that refit came
the first recorded instance of *Victory* having become a tourist attraction. It
was reported that 'boatloads of visitors taken off to visit her'.) And of course

we must not forget the timber shed built to cover No. 3 Slip at Chatham. Built after his retirement but to his design, that awesome timber building is now named after him.

'As long as ships float on the oceon, Sir Robert Seppings will be respected.' (Admiral Sir Thomas Byam Martin during a statement in the House of Commons in 1832)

11
In Memoriam

The contribution Sir Robert Seppings made to shipbuilding history has been recognized in a number of ways; some of which are unusual.

On 6 August 1819, whilst searching for the elusive North-West Passage between the Atlantic and the Pacific, Lieutenant (later Admiral Sir) William Parry in HMS *Hecla* named a cape in Prince Regent Sound in northern Canada after Seppings. Cape Seppings lies in Latitude 73° 48 N, Longitude 90° 20 W. Sir Robert is in distinguished company because Parry named the headland on the other side of the entrance to that Sound, Cape Clarence after HRH The Duke of Clarence, the man who had dubbed Seppings knight.

A hill on an island off the Arakan coast of Myanmar (Burma) is called Seppings Peak. Whether this was named for Sir Robert, or for Edmund Henry Lockyer Seppings a descendent of Sir Robert's brother John, has not been established. Edmund married a Burmese lady Ma Pan Mi in Rangoon in 1893, and died at that place in 1934.

On becoming Surveyor in 1813, and in order to record and show developments in ship design, Robert Seppings established a central ship model room in Somerset House (where it's first curator was a certain Mr. G. Lemon), from Admiralty collections previously held at the various Royal dockyards. Eleven years later, in 1824 King George IV presented thirty portraits of naval commanders to the Seaman's Hospital in Greenwich to augment the modest number it already possessed; they were exhibited in the famous Painted Hall, and the collection came to be known as the Naval Gallery, one of only three public galleries in London at the time. The Seppings' collection of models was soon transferred over to the Naval Gallery as an additional attraction and was exhibited in a neighbouring building. The original collection was enlarged by various gifts, including some from King William IV in 1830, and was further augmented by Seppings' successors. In 1873 the Naval Gallery became known as the Royal Navy Museum and was one of the must-see sights of the city. In his book *Walks in and Around London* published in 1895, the author who called himself 'Uncle Jonathan' wrote, after describing the paintings on show, 'models of ships are amongst the other attractions of the museum here'.

That model collection was enlarged and enhanced again in 1928 when Sir James Caird purchased and then gifted the entire contents of the museum of the Training Ship *Mercury*, which included nearly 200 ship models, fifteen of which were described at the time as 'gems'.[88] The entire collection is now in the keeping of the National Maritime Museum at Greenwich. So, the finest and most extensive collection of ship models in the world had its beginnings with Sir Robert Seppings. (An interesting aside. We have seen how through the marriage of his wife's sister Martha, he was an in-law of the Dacres family. Commander James Richard Dacres of one side of that dynasty, died at Mozambique aged 37 in 1848 when in command of the sloop HMS *Nimrod*. It seems he was a popular officer as subsequently his father, Admiral James Richard Dacres, was presented with a fine model of the *Nimrod* made by two members of its crew in honour of their dead captain. In 1902 Miss Louise Dacres presented the model to the collection at Greenwich.)

A number of Seppings' own models are in the collection at Greenwich. Perhaps an even larger number are in the holdings of the Science Museum at Kensington. A number of European museums have technical models depicting Seppings' shipbuilding methodology, including the Rijksmuseum in Amsterdam and the Musée de la Marine in Paris.

It is an accolade for a person to have a ship named after him or her and, as in this case, the honour is often a posthumous one. The merchant ship *Sir Robert Seppings* of 628 tons was built at Natmoo, near Moulmein, Burma, with all the shipbuilding refinements brought in by the man after whom she was named. She was launched in July 1847. Built of teak, she was made to last. She arrived in London early the following year and on 15 March was put up for auction in the Captains' Room at Lloyds, at that time sited in the Royal Exchange building. During 1850/52 the ship was chartered by

---

[88] The collection was put together by Charles Hoare, the banker who founded the *Mercury* school in 1885. Sir James Caird paid £30,000 for the collection in 1928. The Captain-Superintendent of the *Mercury* for many years was C.B. Fry the famous cricketer. In 1913 the Admiralty loaned the screw-sloop HMS *Gannet* (which had been renamed HMS *President* whilst serving as the HQ ship in the Thames, of the Royal Navy Volunteer Reserve) to the school to be used as a dormitory ship. When the school closed in 1968, that ship returned to the stewardship of the Admiralty. Fully restored and under her original name, HMS *Gannet* is now owned by the Chatham Historic Dockyard.

the British Government as a convict transport and made two voyages to the penal colony at Hobart, Tasmania (at that time still known as Van Diemen's Land). Commanded by Captain Richard Stuart, she sailed from Woolwich on the second of those voyages on 18 March 1852, and after a reasonably fast passage arrived at its destination on 8 July. On board were 220 women convicts – with an average sentence of 8 years transportation – and 21 children aged between 6 and 10. (After that there was only one more such voyage to Hobart – the ship concerned was the *St. Vincent* – before that place ceased to be a transportation destination in 1853.) The *Sir Robert Seppings*, by that time owned by J. Allan of London, then spent the next twenty years trading mainly between Britain and India. Her end came on 2 May 1872 when she was anchored in the Madras roadstead at the time of what has become known as the Great Madras Cyclone. The anchorage was full of ships when this tropical revolving storm struck the port, and the logbook of one of them has survived. Captain Thomas Donkin of the *Inverness* reported for 10 a.m. that day, that the wind was blowing Force 12 with a rapidly falling barometer, and that '*Sir Robert Seppings* seen dragging'; he went on, 'the anchor cables of five other ships have parted'. That storm, in fact, proved to be the end of no less than eleven ships. The *Sir Robert Seppings* was cast ashore, high up on the sands under Fort St. George. She was carrying over 300 people, most of them coolies who were on board to work the cargo. All of them were saved, but many of those aboard other ships were not so lucky. It was reported that there were many, many more casualties amongst the inhabitants of that port-city, many parts of which had been destroyed. The wreck of the *Seppings* was sold by auction for Rupees 7,100 on 10 June, so it is likely some of her long-lasting teak timbers were recycled, as we say nowadays.

At the Great Naval Exhibition held in Chelsea in 1891, the gallery dedicated to naval architecture was called the Seppings Gallery.

In 1922, one of Sir Robert's grandsons bequeathed the Bradley portrait of him to the Royal United Services Institution, along with his grandfather's two gold medals, a cup presented by the Tsar of Russia and a diamond ring presented by William IV. The portrait is now in the keeping of the National Maritime Museum at Greenwich.

More recently, a fine pair of old oak chairs, both fitted with splendidly embroidered cushions, were presented by descendant Faith Packard to St. Mary Magdalene Church in Taunton in memory of her forbears, Sir Robert and Lady Seppings. The chairs are used for brides and grooms at wedding ceremonies. The groom's cushion marked 'Robert', depicts the yacht *Royal George* aboard which he was knighted, and the bride's one, marked 'Charlotte', depicts the couple's house at No. 3 Mount Terrace. Associated with the chairs is a framed document containing copies of portraits of the couple and some bio-information. In 1974 there was a special Service of Dedication in that church when the chairs were handed over.

It has been stated several times in this work, how close the Seppings and Milligen families were and how proud they were of their family connections. Faith Packard seems to have inherited a great deal of that family pride, for in 1973 she made a three-cushion canvas-work sedilia seat for All Saints Church, Shouldham, Norfolk, where John Milligen the draper ended his days. In her book on the family Mrs. Packard indicated that it was also there in honour of Sir Robert Seppings.[89] The seat was dedicated by the Bishop of Ely on 12 June 1973. In the aisle of the church there is a brass plate carrying the following inscription:-

'Hereunder lieth the Body of Mr. John Milligen late of Harleston, linen draper, who died an inhabitant of this Parish, January 27th 1762 aged 68 years. Also Mary Milligen his daughter who died Decr. 16th 1827, aged 94 years.'

The town of Fakenham, Sir Robert's birthplace, unveiled its town sign on 18 November 1978. (Originally planned to form part of the town's celebration of the Queen's Silver Jubilee in 1977, it was delayed by planning permission problems.) The sign is situated at Leach's Corner near the east end of Norwich Street, opposite the old Post Office and within a few yards of the house in which he was born. The sign is T-shaped and double-sided and surmounted by a shield showing a coat of arms. The cross member of the T which carries the town's name, is supported by brackets. The heraldic ship depicted on the side of one of those brackets is there in honour of Sir Robert.

Fakenham was once noted for its printing works, a fact commemorated in a novel fashion on the surface of the pedestrianised part of its market place. It has been laid with facsimile printer's blocks and some of the larger ones depict a stylised sailing vessel under sail. The vessel depicted is a galleon, with a raised forecastle and poop, a type that had disappeared a long time before Sir Robert was born, but that detracts nothing from the fact that they too, are there in his honour.

---

[89] Packard, F., *Our Family History.*

Appendix I
Sir Robert Seppings' Family

Parents

Robert Sepping, b. 1734, Fakenham: d. 1781, Fakenham.
m. Lydia Milligen 29 Jan 1760; b. 1740, Harleston, Suffolk: d. 1821, Fakenham.

Had issue

- John Milligen Seppings, b.1760, Fakenham: d. 1761, Fakenham.
- Lydia Seppings, b. 1762, Fakenham.

  m. (1) 1783, William Sampson. One daughter called Ann b. 1784.

  m. (2) 1790, Green Laws. Three daughters and four sons. The three daughters were Elizabeth b. 1794, Mary b. 1798, and Pleasance. One son, John Milligen b. 1793: d. 1797. See Chapter 7 for details of the other three boys. Lydia died aged 77 in 1838 at Downham Market, Norfolk.

- Mary Seppings, b. 1763, Fakenham; d. 1799.

  m. (1) 1782, Samuel Garrett. One son.

    (2) c.1788, William Brooke Gill, b. 1765, Woodnorton, Norfolk: d. 1839. Four sons, John, William, Thomas, and:

  - Robert, b. 1796, Woodnorton, died 1871, Walton-on-Thames; m. (1) 1838, at Didsbury, Manchester, Frederica Entwistle of the well-to-do Entwistle banking family of Rushholme Hall, near Manchester. She married late in life and died only five years later in July 1843 leaving no issue: (2) 1846, at Mansfield, Notts, Fanny Susannah Need (b. 1821, d. 1911). (Fanny's mother, another Fanny Need, was a wealthy widow by the time of the 1851 Census in which she was described as a land owner. The family wealth came from her father Thomas Need who had made a fortune from timber milling in Canada where he had founded the town of Bobcaygeon in Ontario.)

    Robert Gill and his new wife (25 years his junior), had five children, Frederica (Freda sometimes Freida) Fanny, b.1848, d. 1924; Mary, b.1850, d. 1937; Madeline Lucy, b. 1853, d. 1870; Eleanor Maud, b. 1856, d. 1930, (none of whom married); and the Rev. Robert John Seppings, b.1859, d. 1948 who m. Mary Walters of Llansantffread, Brecon. They had three daughters and a son. One of the daughters., Madeline Francis Gill b.1904, d. 1986, m. 1932, the Rt. Rev. Geoffrey Francis Allen D.D, who was Bishop of Egypt after WW2 before becoming Bishop of Derby. Another of the daughters was Katherine Margaret Gill (see below) b. 1908, d. Surrey, 1995. (She was always known as Margaret.) Robert Gill lived with Sir Robert Seppings and his family at Somerset House in The Strand, London. He had early shown great talent as an engineer and completed his studies whilst living there. He became Sir Robert's favourite nephew and close confidante. Described as a railway pioneer, he was a friend of George Stephenson of *The Rocket* fame and of his son Robert, and of Thomas Longridge Gooch another noted railway engineer. Gill's correspondence with both the Stephensons and with Gooch, together with his other railway records were donated by his granddaughter Margaret Gill to the British Transport Historical Records now in the National Archives at Kew. No doubt using the dowry money from his two marriages, Gill invested heavily in railway shares, and made a fortune. In 1846 a published list of railway subscribers stated that in that year alone he had invested £143,629. (There are indications in Sir Robert's letters that Gill may have borrowed money from him.) Gill's main interests were in the Manchester & Leeds Railway of which he was a Director, and the Lancashire & Yorkshire Railway Company, of which he was Chairman from sometime before 1850. (That is confirmed by an entry in the 1851 Census.) That company with its many spurs and connections, linked Liverpool in the west to Hull in the east, and which for a number of years was the largest railway company in Britain.

According to the Packard Papers he was also one of the moving spirits behind the construction of the Crystal Palace in 1851. The same source also states that he became chairman of the Great Western Railway Company of Canada. The present author has not yet found supporting evidence of either of those claims. By the time of the 1861 Census he and his family were living at Apps Court, Walton-on-Thames in some style with nine servants including a butler and a housekeeper. Freda, his eldest daughter, wrote a *Memoir* about her father. Robert Gill died at Walton-on-Thames in 1871.

- Helen Seppings, b. 1765, Fakenham: d. circa 1859, King's Lynn
  m. 1786, John Pleasance M.D. (1759-1793). They had two daughters, Susan Elizabeth and Mary. Susan, b. 1786, m. at Fakenham, Norfolk, Joseph Dockerill, a Stepney tea merchant in 1815; she d. Islington in 1874. Mary Pleasance married William Beloe in 1816 from whom Edward Milligen Beloe, antiquarian, and author of the biographical article on Sir Robert Seppings in the DNB, was descended.

- Sir Robert Seppings, b. 1767, Fakenham: d. 1840, Taunton, Somerset. m. 1795 at Plymouth, Charlotte Milligen (1770-1834), a first cousin. Had issue:
  * Martha Milligen Seppings, b. 1796, Plymouth: m. 1817, Captain (later Major) James Hull Harrison, R.M. b. 1783, Bombay, d. 1853. The Harrisons had ten children, five boys, five girls. One of the former was Lt. Colonel Robert Seppings Harrison R.M. b. 1822, d. 1872. It was from Robert that Faith Harrison, who married Brigadier J.J. Packard, was descended. Faith Packard privately published a booklet called *Our Family History* in 1989, and Brigadier Packard used some of its information in the Packard Papers held by the National Maritime Museum. (See note below about the Packards.) Martha Harrison d. 1840 at Chapel-en-le-Frith, Derbyshire, probably whilst convalescing in that Peak District town. The following report of her death was published in the *Hampshire Telegraph* on 7 September 1840:
    'Martha Milligen wife of Major Harrison and eldest daughter of the late Sir Robert Seppings, having borne the painful and lingering illness which snatched her in the prime of life from her large and young family.'
  * John Milligen Seppings, b. 1798, Plymouth: d. 1863, Torquay: m.1822, Calcutta, Marianne Matthews, youngest daughter of the late Francis Robert Matthews of Middlesex, (see Chapter 5 for his career information), and had issue,
  - Robert Seymour, b.1825, Calcutta. In the 1871 British Census and again in the 1881 one, he was living at The Cottage, Amesbury and was described as 'an invalid'. He died unmarried aged 70 in 1895 at Cuckfield, Sussex.
  - Edward James, b. 1826, Calcutta. At age seventeen he joined the HEIC Bengal Light Cavalry as a Cornet, (a rank equivalent to an ensign in an infantry regiment). He had risen to lieutenant when on 20 November 1849 he married Jessie Turnbull (daughter of Adam Turnbull and Mary Somerville) at the India Office, Bengal. He was promoted captain in 1855 and in that rank was appointed second-in-command to Major E. Vibart of the 2nd Bengal Light Cavalry stationed at Cawnpore, a railway town on the banks of the River Ganges, in 1857. By that time the couple had three infant sons, John James born 1852, Edward Matthew in 1854, and a still unnamed boy who was only a week or two old when the so-called Indian Mutiny began in June 1857. During what became known as the Seige of Cawnpore and the

ensuing massacre there, several hundred Europeans including that entire branch of the Seppings' family lost their lives, the Seppings baby being the youngest of all the victims. Most of the civilians, including Jesse and her children, were thrown alive down a well. Edward and other captured soldiers were slaughtered on the banks of the Ganges.

This sad story is mentioned in detail here to show that Edward James Seppings was Sir Robert's grandson and not his son as recorded in both the first and second editions of the British Dictionary of National Biography. The initial error was made by Edward Milligen Beloe, a distant family member, a mistake perpetuated by David K. Brown in the DNB revised edition.

It is also mentioned because the death of Edward and his three sons in 1857 meant that when Edward's unmarried brother Robert died in 1895, there were no male heirs to carry on the Seppings surname in Sir Roberts's branch of the family. All his other many descendants stem from female lines.

Between 1858 and 1862 John Milligen Seppings contributed funds towards the rebuilding of the Taunton church in which his parents had worshipped after their retirement.

- Charlotte Marianne, b. 1828, Calcutta. Married William Bentinck Forfar (d. 1895, Bournemouth) in 1868 at Redruth in Cornwall. Charlotte Marianne d. in 1894.
- Mary Milligen Seppings, b. 1799, Plymouth: d. 1879, Exeter: m. Dr. Robert Armstrong (1796-1855), a naval surgeon, in 1832 in London. They had two sons, and two daughters. After joining the naval service in 1816 Armstrong served as surgeon superintendent on three convict ships to New South Wales between 1818 and 1822. They were the *Tottenham, Dick*, and *Countess of Harcourt*. Of the total of 692 convicts shipped out under his care, he lost only 13, a remarkably low figure compared to most other such voyages, and 10 of those died of scurvy aboard the first of those ships whose voyage out had been prolonged by adverse weather. He gained his M.D. at Edinburgh in 1825, and after service in various naval vessels, was appointed surgeon to the Plymouth Naval Hospital in 1829. He published a book on the cause and prevention of diseases to seamen in 1843, that included an account of fevers prevalent in the West Indies. He was appointed Inspector of Hospitals and Fleets in 1847. He died at Hill's Court in Exeter in 1855.
- Richard Nankivel Seppings, b. 1801, Plymouth: d. 1802, Plymouth.

* Charlotte Lucy Seppings, b. 1803, Chatham: d. 1809, Chatham.
* Andrew Sanders Seppings, b. 1806, Chatham: an invalid, he never married: d. 1849, Pembroke. (See Chapter 7.)
* Robert Richard Seppings, b. 1807, Chatham: d. 1807, Chatham.
* Lydia Milligen Seppings, b. 1807, Chatham: d. 1807, Chatham.
* Louisa Seppings, b. 1810, Chatham: d. 1891,Dudley, Worcs. (See Chapter 10.)
* Helen Seppings, b. 1812, Chatham: m. Daniel Godfrey (of Abingdon and a solicitor) 1837, at Taunton. They had eight children. One of their sons, Robert Seppings Godfrey became Registrar of the Supreme Court in London in 1899. The youngest daughter Georgina Francis deserves a mention here because the notice of her marriage to George Thorne-George that appeared in London's *Morning Post* on 30 April 1883, showed that the family were still proud of their Seppings' connection, by stating that she was the granddaughter of Sir Robert Seppings who had by then been dead for over 50 years. Georgina d. 1928 at Chelsea.
* John Milligen Seppings, b. 1770, Fakenham: d. 1826, Chudleigh, Devon: m. 1804, Ann Maria Marshall Lockyer at Plymouth. Ann was born in Plymouth in 1782, and died at Exeter in 1859. Eleven children. (See Chapter 7 for details of the five boys who were all helped by Sir Robert.) The six girls were:
  • Ann Maria Swainson, b. 1806, Greenwich: d. 1863, Newton Abbot, Devon. m. Rev. Cummings. One daughter who m. a Canon Syers.
  • Clara Louisa, b. 1814, Greenwich: d. 1817, Greenwich.
  • Eliza Jane Bicknell, b. 1815, Greenwich: d. 1854, Chudleigh, Devon. m. 1843 Thomas Yarde. One son, one daughter.
  • Emily Elizabeth, b. 1819, Greenwich: d. 1835, Plymouth.
  • Augusta Mary, b. 1820, Chudleigh: d. 1910, Okehampton, Devon. She m. the Rev. Edward Puttock in 1855. He died in 1880. They had five children. The eldest son Edward Henry Puttock b.1857: d. 1897. He m. Alice Cluff and had five children. The youngest, Mary Katherine Puttock b. 1897: d.1948. She m. Richard Townley Colthurst. They had two daughters, one son. The son, Christopher John Seppings Colthurst b. 1933: d. 1998. Many of the Seppings family portraits ended up in his possession.
  • Charlotte Ellis, b. 1822, Chudleigh: m. George Oxenham, 1858: d. 1880, London.
  • Elizabeth Seppings, b. 1774, Fakenham: m. Robinson Cornish. Two children, Thomas and William.

Note on the Packards

Mary Faith Harrison, always called Faith, was born at Marylebone, London, in 1919. She was the daughter of George H. Harrison and Bessie Brooks who married at Wandsworth, London in that same year. Faith was the great-great-granddaughter of Martha Milligen, Sir Robert Seppings' eldest daughter, and so was a direct descendant. She died at Tower Hamlets, London, in 2003. In addition to writing *Our Family History*, published in 1989, she was responsible for placing the Seppings' commemorative chairs, cushions and the associated plaque in the Parish Church in Taunton.

Faith married at Kensington in 1942, Joseph John Packard. Born in 1910 in Belfast where his father was serving in the army; he enlisted in the army in 1928 and served in the ranks for 3 years and 133 days according to the Army List of 1939, before being commissioned as 2nd Lieutenant in the East Yorkshire Regiment in January 1932. He was a full lieutenant when he sailed with other officers to Bombay in the P&O ship *Moolton*, from London on 24 September 1935. He was back in England in 1937 and was promoted Captain in May 1939. In 1939 he was listed as 'specially employed' and was mentioned in despatches. In 1945 he was a temporary Lt. Colonel and was confirmed in that rank in 1952. Served in the Korean War. Later served as Military Attaché in Vienna. In 1959 he was posted in the rank of Brigadier to Berlin as Chief of the British Mission to the Russians. He retired from the army in 1961. Compiler of the Packard Papers in the National Archives at Kew, he also wrote articles for learned journals.

The Packards had five children, Peter John, b. 1943; Mark Anthony Clive, b.1947; Mary Anne Faith, b. 1949; Timothy Paul, b. 1952; and Simon David, b. 1955. Mary Ann Faith, married in 1985 at Westminster, Randal H. I. Gray. (b. 1952.) They had one son, Rowland Hewett Gray, born 1989. Mary died in 2015. Her obituary read,

'Mary Ann Faith Gray nee Packard, suddenly at home 24 April 2015, aged 66 years. Beloved wife of Randal and mother of Rowland, daughter of the late Brigadier J.J. Packard and Faith Packard. Funeral at St. Peter's, North Hill, Colchester, 9 June 2015.'

Appendix II

This document, signed by Robert Seppings presents a list of his inventions and improvements up to the time he was knighted on 24 March 1819.

To H.R.H. the Prince Regent, dated 1st March 1819.
Surveyor of His Majesty's Navy:
"Sheweth, - That your Royal Highness's memorialist, on 26th August 1800, proposed an alteration to be made in the braces and pintles, or mode of hanging ships' rudders, to remedy the inconvenience, and to prevent the expense, arising in consequence of the wearing away of their crowns by the action of the rudder, which was immediately adopted, and generally introduced in His Majesty's dock-yards per Navy Board warrant dated 28th August 1800.

"That your Royal Highness's memorialist, on 1st January 1801, proposed a plan for removing blocks from under ships in dock, to enable the workmen to remedy defects in ships' keels, to make additions thereto, or to caulk the garboard or lower seams of the bottom, without lifting the ships. The advantage of this plan in the saving of expense and labour were so obvious that the Lords Commissioners of the Admiralty, by their letter dated 5th February 1803, ordered it to be generally introduced in His Majesty's yards, and as a reward for this invention, your Royal Highness's memorialist was presented with £1000 by Government, and a gold medal from the Society of Arts.

"That your Royal Highness's memorialist, on the 13th February 1806, proposed a plan for scarphing straight timber to obtain a compass form, by the adoption of which the Warspite, of 74 guns, (which although ordered to be built many years could not be proceeded with for the want of compass timber) was completed in twenty-one months, including six months for seasoning: the other advantages arising from the adoption of this plan, are that of giving a ship's frame an equal degree of seasoning, which was heretofore unavoidably composed of a mixture of seasoned and unseasoned materials by which the timber in the same ship had different periods of durability, thereby occasioning rapid decay. The importance of this plan was so obvious that it has been introduced in His Majesty's dock-yards, by order of the Navy Board, dated 1st January 1808.

"That your Royal Highness's memorialist, on 28th May 1807, proposed a plan to build round bows to ships of the line, which gives great additional strength to the ship, more convenience and comfort to the crew, and security in time of action. The superiority of this plan was so apparent that it has been generally introduced in His Majesty's navy, by directions from the Lords Commissioners of the Admiralty dated 29th May 1811.

"That your Royal Highness's memorialist, in the early part of the year 1800, partially introduced a plan of laying materials diagonally in His Majesty's ship Glenmore of 36 guns; and on 19th May 1805 proposed a similar introduction of materials in the Kent of 74 guns, in consequence of her extraordinary defects arising from weakness, of which the Navy Board approved by their warrant dated 4th June, 1805.

"The advantages which resulted from a partial introduction of the diagonal system induced your Royal Highness's memorialist , on 5th February 1810, to propose that it should be fully carried into effect in the construction and repairs of His Majesty's ships, which has been the cause of a total change in our national bulwark, by the introduction of a diagonal trussed frame, the filling in of the spaces between the timbers below the orlop deck with wood and cement, a new mode of attaching the beams to the sides, laying the decks diagonally, and by omitting a considerable quantity of materials hitherto unnecessarily or injudiciously applied: the furtherance of this plan, and the bringing it to maturity by furnishing drawings, rules, regulations, and by giving active personal inspection, have been the labour of nearly nineteen years, by which the health of your Royal Highness's memorialist has been much injured, and his domestic comforts much interfered with. The results of this plan, generally introduced by the Lords Commissioners of the Admiralty, dated 29th October 1812, are, economy in the construction or repairs of His Majesty's ships, by a saving of a considerable quantity of scarce and valuable timber, and substituting old ship-timber and new timber of inferior quality and lengths in its stead, which is peculiarly applicable to the new principle, and in many instances carried to a considerable extent. It is difficult to make any calculation of the saving to the public by the increased durability of the ships, and the saving of materials to a considerable amount, great strength however is obtained, and the health of their crews promoted (with regard to the latter, see Sir Gilbert Blane's "Treatise on the Health of the Navy"). All these have been proved by the severe trials to which several of the ships have been put, which have been constructed on this principle, and the success of which induced the Royal Society, in 1818, to honour your Royal Highness's memorialist with their gold medal. The account of this new principle of ship-building is published in the "Transactions of the Royal Society", in 1814 and 1818.

"That your Royal Highness's memorialist, on the 12th April 1812, proposed to construct a sheer-hulk for Chatham yard, with strait [sic] fir timber, preventing thereby the consumption of much valuable compass oak timber, and causing a considerable saving of expense. The Lords Commissioners of the Admiralty, by their order dated 1st May 1812, approved of this proposition being adopted, and the hulk has been found fully to answer the purposes for which it was constructed.

"That from the great accumulation of small or frigates' timber in the several dock-yards remarked by the Lords Commissioners of the Admiralty, on their visitation in the year 1813, your Royal Highness's memorialist, on the 5th November of that year, proposed a plan for building ships of the line with timber hitherto considered applicable only to frigates, and applying that which was fit only for inferior uses to principal purposes; it also obviates the necessity of using compass timber for floors, transoms, etc. The expense of the frame of the Thunderer (now named Talavera) built on this principle by directions of the Lords Commissioners of the Admiralty, dated 28th February 1814, and lately launched at Woolwich, is £900 less than that of the Black Prince, a ship of similar dimensions, built on the old principle. This method of connecting the timbers was the ground work of the present mode of framing in the British navy, by introducing the same union of materials in the ships built with large, that had been applied to small timber; and decreasing thereby, very considerably, the consumption of timber, and rendering the ships much stronger, as was ascertained by a trial of the frames of the before mentioned ships.

"That your Royal Highness's memorialist, on 25th April 1815, proposed a plan for making top-masts by scarphing or lengthening the sticks below the cap, and substituting those of less dimensions, consequently of much less value. These have on trial, been found fully to answer the intended purpose, as appears by a letter from Sir Benjamin Hallowell to the Navy Board, dated 28th July 1818, enclosing a report from the captain and carpenter of the Ramillies, dated the 24th of the same month, in which ship they have been in use upwards of three years, and are still in good state. The saving produced by the adoption of this proposition, although considerable, is of little moment, in comparison with the inconvenience and delay before experienced for the want of the article, which in many instances, could not be procured but with the greatest difficulty. The Lords Commissioners of the Admiralty directed the introduction of this plan on 3rd February 1819.

"That your Royal Highness's memorialist, on 7th June 1816, proposed a plan for the introduction of circular sterns to ships, which causes a great increase of strength, forms a more extensive and efficient battery in the stern for attack or defence, affords protection when raked, prevents injury from explosion in firing the guns, gives a facility of working those in the stern equal to those in the sides, - in fact renders that part of a ship capable of making resistance which was heretofore defenceless. In the event of a ship being pooped, no evil can arise; and, if required, the ship may be moored by the stern. With these advantages the consumption of compass timber is decreased. The general introduction of this plan was directed by order of the Lords Commissioners of the Admiralty, dated 13th June 1817.

"That your Royal Highness's memorialist, on 17th July 1816, proposed a new method of raising the lower masts of ships out of their steps, by means of a simple and portable apparatus of his invention, which requires only four men to raise a first rate's mainmast, instead of about ninety. The adoption of this method has rendered two sheer-hulks unnecessary, one at Portsmouth, and one in Plymouth, which had been kept up at an annual expense of nearly £2000. It has also, by the removal of the hulk lying at Plymouth to Sheerness, where one was required, caused an immediate saving of £14,000, the expense incurred in fitting the Sampson sheer-hulk at Woolwich; and a similar sum would have been required to fit a sheer-hulk for Portsmouth, in lieu of the Neptune, which had been found so defective as to render it necessary to take her to pieces. In a series of years, this expense must again have been incurred (when from age or accident the hulks required replacing), which is now prevented. The risk and expense of moving either ship or hulk, which was before necessary, is avoided by this apparatus. The heels of the mast (resting on a pig of ballast) can thus at all times be examined (instead of being lifted as heretofore triennially, at a very considerable expense), and the decay occasioned by their being stepped in the mortices prevented. This causes a saving beyond calculation. This proposition was approved of by the Lords Commissioners of the Admiralty, 2nd September 1816.

"That your Royal Highness's memorialist, on 8th October 1816, proposed a plan for mooring ships in Ordinary with chain slip bridles, which affords a more easy way of extricating the ships from their moorings in case of fire, or the necessity of moving them from any cause, as well as removing a most injurious weight from their bows. It will cause a saving in mooring ships in Ordinary of nearly one half of the quantity of chain, amounting in value to no less than £10,000; and, from the frequent necessity of changing the hempen bridles (where used) by their rapid deterioration to prevent accidents to ships, will occasion an annual saving of some thousands of pounds.

"That your Royal Highness's memorialist, on 27th January 1817, presented a plan for substituting iron chain or rods for harbour rigging, in lieu of cordage, which on adoption has caused a very considerable saving of expense; and a still further saving will be produced annually by the durability of iron compared with that of rope. It also tends much to put a stop to extensive embezzlements. Its introduction was directed by the Navy Board's warrant dated 5th February 1817.

"That your Royal Highness's memorialist, on 5th September 1817, proposed a plan for reducing the length of the timbers of a ship's frame, and doing away with the chocks at their heads and heels, which chocks not only produce decay as it respects themselves, but infests the timbers with which they come in contact. The introduction by your Royal Highness's memorialist, of coaks, and working the timbers with square heads and heels, has given a strength and connection hitherto unknown until introduced in the frame of the Thunderer (now Talavera). The simplicity of the workmanship, and economy in the conversion of timber, although of considerable moment, are of trifling importance compared with the plan of rendering timber generally more applicable to the frames of ships, which heretofore was only partially so, and causing them to possess greater strength and durability. As proof of the utility of the plan, two 28-gun ships are now constructing solely of fir timber, which never was before done by any mode of framing, as considerable quantities of oak and elm timber were before introduced in the construction of what were termed fir frigates. This plan is generally introduced in all classes of His Majesty's ships by directions from the Lord Commissioners of the Admiralty, dated 4th February 1818.

"That your Royal Highness's memorialist, on 15th January 1819, proposed a plan for the introduction of iron laid diagonally, instead of wood in frigates, which will cause considerable durability to the ships, and prevent the consumption of much useful timber. It will also give greater room for stowage, shorten the fastenings, and consequently give increased strength.

This plan has been directed to be introduced by order of the Lords Commissioners of the Admiralty, dated 23rd January 1819.

"That your Royal Highness's memorialist was apprenticed in March 1782, to Sir John Henslow, late Surveyor of His Majesty's Navy, who was then Master Shipwright of Plymouth yard; and was at a considerable expense to his friends during that apprenticeship, and by regular gradations, after more than thirty-one years, arrived at the situation which he now fills, making at this time a servitude of thirty-seven years. That your Royal Highness's memorialist has had no pecuniary or other advantage (except in one instance as herein stated) for the numerous inventions and improvements which are here detailed, and for others of minor consideration, which have been introduced in His Majesty's naval service, notwithstanding such immense sums have been saved to the public by the adoption of the plans of your Royal Highness's memorialist, and on which Government have expended, and are expending, to the amount of some millions of money; and that in point of fact he sacrificed comfort and gained no emolument (as stated by the Select Committee of Finance in their 6th Report, page 190), by leaving the situation of Master Shipwright of Chatham dock-yard, and accepting that of Surveyor of His Majesty's navy, and which he was induced to do only from the consideration that he would be empowered thereby to protect those plans which he had brought forward, and to introduce others for the good of His Majesty's service. Models, drawings, and descriptions of the several inventions herein detailed, are in possession of your Royal Highness's memorialist, which will more fully explain what he has endeavoured to describe.

"Your Royal Highness's memorialist therefore prays that your Royal Highness will be pleased to take into consideration the many and important services that he has rendered to his Country, with the heavy responsibility he incurred in carrying his plans into execution; and that your Royal Highness will be graciously pleased to confer on him such reward as your Royal Highness may consider him deserving."

(Signed) R. Seppings.

Bibliography

Books

Anon, *The Historic Dockyard, Chatham*, Chatham Dockyard Trust, 1994

Banbury, Philip, *Shipbuilders of the Thames & Medway,* David & Charles, Newton Abbot, 1971

Barrow, Sir John, *A Family Tour Through South Holland*, John Murray, London 1831

Blomefield, F., *History of Norfolk*, circa 1806

Boudriot, Jean, *The Seventy-Four Gun Ships*, 4 vols. Collection Archeologie Navale Francaise, Paris, 1986

Boxer, C.R., *The Portuguese Seaborne Empire*, 1415-1825, Hutchinson, London, 1969

Brindley, Robert, *Naval Architecture arranged in Q's and A's*, Sherwood, Gillett & Piper, London, 1832

Bulley, Anne, *Free Mariner, John Adolphus Pope, 1786-1821,* BACSA, London, 1992

Carter, H.B., *Sir Joseph Banks*, British Museum, London, 1988

Clements, Paul, *Marc Isambard Brunel*, Longmans, London, 1970

Coad, Jonathan, *Historic Architecture of the Royal Navy,* Gollancz, London, 1983

Colledge, J.J., *Ships of the Royal Navy*, 2 vols, David & Charles, Newton Abbot, 1969-1970

Davidson, James, *Admiral Lord St. Vincent, Sailor or Sinner*, Pen & Sword, Barnsley, 2007

Dictionary of National Biography, 1st & 2nd. Editions.

Fincham, J., *History of Naval Architecture*, London, 1851

Forester, C.S., *The Naval War of 1812*, Michael Joseph, London, 1957

Fry, C.B., *Life Worth Living,* Eyre & Spottiswoode, London, 1939

Goodwin, Peter, *The Ships of Trafalgar*, Conway, London, 2005

Harrod, Dominick ed., *War, Ice & Piracy*, Chatham, London, 2000

Haas, J. M., *A Management Odyssey: The Royal Dockyards, 1714-1914*,
   University Press of America, Lanham. Maryland, 1994
Holland, A.J., *Ships of British Oak*, David & Charles, Newton Abbot, 1971
   Buckler's Hard, Kenneth Mason, Emsworth, 1985
Horsley, John E., *Tools of the Maritime Trades*, David & Charles, Newton
   Abbot, 1978
Horten, Brian, *HMS Trincomalee*, Profile, Windsor, 1979

Knowles, John, *Appendix on the Principles & Practices of Constructing the
   Royal & Mercantile Navies Invented by Sir Robert Seppings*, London, 1822

Lambert, Andrew, *The Last Sailing Battle Fleet*, London, 1991
Landstrom. Bjorn, *The Ship*, Allen & Unwin, London, 1961
Lees, James, The Masting & Rigging of English Ships of War 1625-1860,
   Conway, Greenwich, 1971
Lloyd, Christopher, *Captain Marryat and the Old Navy*, Longman's Green,
   London, 1939
Lubbock, Basil, *The Blackwall Frigates*, Brown, Son & Ferguson,
   Glasgow, 1924

MacGregor, David R., *Merchant Sailing Ships 1815-1850*, Conway,
   London, 1984
Marryat, Florence, *Life and Letters of Captain Marryat*, 2 vols, 1872
Marsh, A.J., *The Story of a Frigate*, Portsmouth Museum Society, 1982
Mcllwain, John, *HMS Trincomalee*, Pitkin, Andover, 1994
Money, W.T., *The Expediency of Shipbuilding at Bombay*, Longman,
   London, 1811

Packard, Faith, *Our Family History*, self-published, 1989
Phipps, John, *A Collection of Papers Related to Shipbuilding in India*,
   Calcutta, 1840
Platts, Beryl, *History of Greenwich*, 1973
Pocock, Tom, *Captain Marryat: Seaman, Writer, & Adventurer*, Chatham,
   London, 2000

Skempton, A.W., et al, *A Biographical Dictionary of Civil Engineers in Great
   Britain and Ireland*, 2002
Steel, David, *Elements & Practice of Naval Architecture*, London, 1805
Sutherland, R.J.M., *Structural Iron, 1750-1850*, Routledge, London, 1997

Sutton, Jean, *Lords of the East: The East India Company & its Ships*,
    Conway, Greenwich, 1981
Syrett, D. & DiNardo, R.L., eds. *Commissined Sea Officers of the Royal Navy*
    1660-1815, Navy Record Society, 1994

Walker, F.M., *Ships and Shipbuilders: Pioneers of Design & Construction*,
    Seaforth, Barnsley, 2010
Warner, Oliver, *Captain Marryat, A Rediscovery*, Constable, London, 1953
Winfield, Rif, *British Warships in the Age of Sail 1603-1714*, Seaforth,
    Barnsley, 2009
    British Warships in the Age of Sail 1714-1792, Seaforth, Barnsley, 2007
    British Warships in the Age of Sail 1793-1817, Seaforth, Barnsley, 2005

Articles and Theses
Albion, Robert G., *The Timber Problem of the Royal Navy, 1652-1862*,
    Mariner's Mirror, Vol. 38, No.1, 1952

Cunningham, Surgeon L.S., *Day Book*, File ADM101/68/4/1-9,
    National Archives, Kew
Flynn, Peter Erik, *HMS Pallas: Historical Reconstruction of an 18th C. Royal*
    Navy Frigate, MA thesis, Texas A&M University, 2006
Fraser, Edward, *British Watercraft – HMS Victory (1765)*, Mariner's Mirror,
    Vol. 8 No. 4, 1922

Lambert, Andrew, *The Reconstruction of the Royal Navy, 1815-1830*,
    Mariner's Mirror, 1996
Lemmars, Alan, *Shipworm, Hogbacks and Duck's Arses: the Influence of William*
    May on Sir Robert Seppings, Mariner's Mirror, Vol.99, No.4, 2013

MacDougall, Philip, article in Lunn & Day's *History of Labour in the Royal*
    Dockyards
Macleod, N., *The Shipwrights of the Royal Dockyards*, Mariner's Mirror,
    Vol. 11, No. 3, 1925
Marryat, Frederick, aka 'FM', *The School of Naval Architecture*, United
    Services Journal, Part 1, 1834
Morriss, R.A., *Labour Relations in the Royal Dockyards 1801-05*, Mariner's
    Mirror, Vol. 82, 1976

'Nauticus', *Sir Charles Vinicombe Penrose*, Mariner's Mirror, Vol.29,
    No.2. 1943

Packard, J.J., *Sir Robert Seppings and the Timber Problem*, Mariner's Mirror, Vol. 64, No. 2, 1978

Rice, William McPherson, *A Key-fid for Striking Topmasts and Top-Gallant masts: and for Adjusting the Shrouds to a Proper Degree of Tension, Without Slacking the Laniards*, United Services Journal, No. 37, December 1831.

Seppings, John Milligen, treatise, *Indian Timber and Shipbuilding*, (in Phipps, see above), Calcutta, 1837.
Seppings, Robert, *On the great strength given to Ships of War by the application of Diagonal Bracing*, Philosophical Transactions, Royal Society, 1817

Tilloch, Alexander, *Mr. Seppings' Method of Suspending Ships*, Philosophical Magazine, No.22, XXXVI, London, 1804
Tripati, S., et al, *Role of Teak and Other Hardwoods in Shipbuilding*, Current Science, Vol. III, No. 7, October 2016

Newspapers and Periodicals
Illustrated London News
Naval & Military Gazette, London
Morning Post, London
Globe, London
Cheltenham Chronicle
Kentish Gazette
Hampshire Advertiser
Dorset County Chronicle
Caledonian Mercury
The Metropolitan Magazine
East-India Register & Army List
Taunton Courier & Advertiser
Newcastle Journal
Maidstone Journal
Bell's Weekly Messenger, London
Western Times, Devon
Public Ledger & Daily Advertiser
London Courier & Evening Gazette
Cornishman
Bath Chronicle
Naval Chronicle
United Services Journal
Colburne's *United Service Gazette* 1858, Part II
Monthly Magazine & British Register, 1822
Gravesend & Dartford Reporter
European Magazine & London Review, 1799

National Archives
ADM37/8340; ADM1/2205/49; ADM1/2205/55; ADM52 Masters' logbooks

Internet sources
HathiTrust
Haileybury ex-East India College records

Index

Adams, Henry, Shipbuilder, 8
Anderson, Master Painter. Seppings secures an award for, 47
Austen, Captain Francis R.N. 16; 33

Banks, Sir Joseph, 48; 73
Barrow, Sir James, 28; 34, 44/5; 73
Battle of Trafalgar, 30
Beloe, Edward Milligen, 4; 93/4
Brooking, Rear Admiral Samuel, 85, 90-92
Buckler's Hard, 8
Byam Martin, Rear Admiral Sir
>Thomas, 48; & timber problem 61; attempts to obtain reward for Seppings, 70/2; dismissal of, 93

Cape Seppings, Canada, 110
Chapman, Fredrik Henrik, Swedish Shipbuilder, 42 n.30
Clarence, HRH Duke of, 35; confers knighthood on Seppings, 49; 75; 106
'Compass' timbers, 11, 59
Compression & Tension forces on ship structures, 22/3
Congo affair, 73/4
Consanguineous marriages, 24
Cotton, Joseph, on teak-built ships 68

Dacres, Lady Martha nee Milligen, 5
Davy, Sir Humphry, 65/6
Ditchburn, Thomas, one of Seppings' apprentices, 51
Ditchburn & Mare, Thames shipbuilders, 51

Dockyard apprentice training & duties, 9-12
Dupin, Charles, French naval engineer, 29

Experimental Squadrons, 80 et seq.

Fakenham town tributes to Seppings, 113
'Fir frigates', 23
Fletcher & Fearnall, Thames Shipbuilders, 51
Fuseli, Henry, painter, 24 n.5
Fryer, John, Master R.N., 21/2; 30

Gill, Frieda, her description of Lady Charlotte Seppings, 57
Gill, Robert, (nephew of Sir Robert) 97/8; 99
Graham, Sir James, First Lord of the Admiralty, 93; on Symond's time in office, 95

Hardy, Admiral Thomas M., 30
Hayes, Captain John R.N., 76; 77
Hayward, William J., apprenticed to Seppings, 13
Henslow, Sir John, Surveyor of the Navy, Robert Seppings apprenticed to, 7; career outline, 7/8; 12; 37
Heywood, Captain Peter R.N., 33
Hohlenberg, Franz, Danish shipbuilder, 44

Inman, Rev. James, Principal of School of Naval Architectur 49/50; 76

Jervis, Admiral John, Lord
  St. Vincent, 19-21; 60

Keene, Captain Robert R.N., 15; 17
Knowles, John, Chief Clerk to the
  Surveyor of the Navy, 23/4; n. 15;
  28; 40 n.25;
  on Seppings' achievements, 45/6

Labour relations in HM dockyards,
  14; 18
Laws, Rear Admiral John, 76/7
Lock, Sir Joseph, knighted in error,
  105/6
Lock, Mrs Louisa nee Seppings, 105

Mathias, Charles Esq., 79
Mare, C.J., Thames shipbuilders,
  51
Marryat, Captain Frederick R.N.,
  99 et seq
May, Captain William, Dutch
  shipbuilder, 42 et seq
Milligen, John, draper 3
Milligen, Captain John R.N., 3; 4;
  career outline 5/6; 7; 9;
  death of, 12
Mould Loft, in shipyard, description
  of, 11

Naval War of 1812, 37
Nelson, Vice Admiral Lord Horatio,
  8; 17; 29

Packard, Faith, 3n; 112/13
Palmer, John, apprenticed to
  Seppings 13
Parkins, George, Master Shipwright
  at Chatham post-Seppings, 31
Penrose, Vice Admiral Sir Charles,
  84/5
Phipps, John. of HEIC Master
  Attendant's Office, Calcutta, 55

Puget, Rear Admiral Peter, 6
Plymouth Breakwater, 21

Rennie, John, 21; 73
Rice, William McPherson, 50; 51
Rivers, Midshipman William, 31
Roberts, Midshipman Richard, 30/1
Royal School of Naval Architecture
  and Marine Engineering, 96
Royal Society, 48
Rule, Sir William, Surveyor of the
  Navy, 8

School of Naval Architecture,
  founding of, 49/50; 96
'Seppings Effect', 21
Seppings' Gallery, 112
Seppings' Peak, Burma, 110
Seppings, Lt. John Milligen R.N.
  (Sir Robert's brother), adoption, 5;
  naval career 6;
  marriage, 12; 85-89
Seppings, John Milligen (Seppings'
  son), HEIC Surveyor, 13; 50-56
Seppings, Lady Charlotte, 5; 12; 24;
  description of, 57;
  death of, 105
Seppings, Mrs. Lydia (Seppings'
  mother), 3; 7; 10; 26
Seppings, Lydia (Seppings' sister),
  adoption 5; 7
Seppings, Sir Robert, birth & early
  childhood 3;
  education 4; mule mail service, 4;
  his adoption, 5; apprenticed to
  Henslow 7;
  apprenticeship training 9-12;
  career at Plymouth 12;
  appointed Assistant Master
  Shipwright, Plymouth, 14;
  'Seppings' Blocks' 15-19;

appointed Master Shipwright,
Chatham, 25 et seq;
experiments in strengthening
ship structures, 27 et seq;
new bow design, 32 et seq;
promotion to Surveyor, 35 et seq;
and Copley Medal, 38; patents
his fid apparatus, 51/2;
prosecutes servant, 56;
death of mother, 57;
and timber problem 58 et seq;
iron for wood substitution, 59;
and Marc Brunel, 61/3;
HMS Eden experiment, 64;
and copper-sheathing, 64 et seq;
and Sir Humphry Davy, 65;
his steamships, 73/4; and the
experimental squadrons, 76 et seq;
on his shipbuilding principles, 84;
his criticisms of his brother's
family, 85; in litigation, 89/90;
his dismissal from office, 93-95;
retirement to Somerset, 97;
Vivary, 97; Whidbey litigation, 98;
Bradley portrait, 99; 112;
Knight portrait 99; his exchanges
with Captain Marryat 102/3;
the ships constructed by him, 104;
visit to HMS Rodney, 106;
death of, 107;
his role in establishing the ship
model collection in the NMM,
110/11
Seppings, Robert senior, 3; 5
Smith, Reverend Sydney, 93
Symonds, Captain Sir William R.N.,
76; 77; 95/6
Ships
(Royal Navy)
Abundance 30

Acorn 76
Agamemnon 8; 17
Anson 8
Ariadne 103/4
Barham 96
Bellona 40
Bounty 21; 35
Caledonia 33/5
Cambridge 44
Canopus 16; 19
Castor 96; 102
Champion 76; 77
Chatham 61
Christian VII 44
Columbia 51
Columbine 76
Comet 75
Confiance 97
Congo 75
Culloden 59
Defence 17
Discovery 6; 21
Duke of Kent 35 n.21
Dunkirk 6
Eagle 6
Eden 64
Fly 7
Ganges 51; 75; n.60
Gannet 51
Glenmore 23
Glory 17
Hercules 35
Howe 35; 66
Impregnable 27; 60
Iphigenia 27
Java 37
Kent 28; 40; 43
Leyden 43
Lively 35
Justitia 49

Medusa 8
Mersey 58/9
Meleager 27
Minotaur 35
Nimrod 61
Orlando 27
Orestes 76
Penelope 6
Pique 96
Pyramus 76
Ramilles 60
Revenge 27
Rodney 106
Royal George (yacht) 49
Royal Sovereign 8; 12
San Josef 15
Sapphire 76
Satellite 76; 77-79
Spartiate 50
Spitfire 15; 17
Sybille 76
Terror 51
Tonnant 59
Tremendous 29
Trincomalee 37
Tweed 23
Tyne 83/4
Unicorn 66; 69
Vernon 96; 102
Victory 7; 29-32; 58
Ville de Paris 6
Warrior, ironclad, 51; 96
Warspite 27; 60
(British merchant)
HEIC Cowasjee 55
HEIC Ganges 54
HEIC George Canning 51
HEIC Hoogly 55
HEIC Irawaddy 54
HEIC Rob Roy 55

HEIC Sylph 55
HEIC Warren Hastings 54; 75
HEIC William Money 53
Sir Robert Seppings 111/2
(Others ships)
Christian VII (Danish navy) 44
USS Constitution 37
Le Franklin (French navy) 16
Leiden (Dutch navy) 43,
Samuel Smith, U.S. schooner 103/4

Shaffhausen Bridge, 38
Slade, Benjamin, shipbuilder, 8
Slade, Sir Thomas, shipbuilder, 7
Snodgrass, Gabriel, HIEC Surveyor,
    8; 39-42
Somerset House, Naval Board
    Offices, 36 et seq

Thames Ironworks & Shipbuilding
    Co. Ltd., 51/2
Tilloch, Alexander, 15 et seq
Treatise on Indian shipbuilding
    timbers, 55
Tucker, Joseph, Surveyor of the
    Navy, 12; 14; 35 n.21

Vancouver, Captain George R.N.,
    6; 21

Wadia, Jamsetjee Bomanjee, Bombay
    shipbuilder, 37
Walker, Admiral Sir Baldwin Wake,
    96
Watt, James jnr., 73
Watts, Isaac, Chief Constructor, 96
Wells, Vice Admiral Thomas, 17
Whidbey, Joseph, Master R.N.,
    21/2; 97/8

Yorke, Charles, First Lord of the
    Admiralty, 28

Printed in Great Britain
by Amazon

87474099R00090